DEBRETT'S

Guide to
ENTERTAINING
ETIQUETTE

First published in Great Britain in 2013 by Simon & Schuster UK Ltd
A CBS COMPANY

10 9 8 7 6 5 4 3 2 1

SIMON & SCHUSTER ILLUSTRATED BOOKS
Simon & Schuster UK Ltd
222 Gray's Inn Road
London
WC1X 8HB

www.simonandschuster.co.uk

Simon & Schuster Australia, Sydney

Simon & Schuster India, New Delhi

A CIP catalogue record for this book is available
from the British Library

ISBN: 978-1-47110-155-7

Printed and bound in China

DEBRETT'S

Text
Jo Bryant
Elizabeth Wyse

Editorial
Jo Bryant
Elizabeth Wyse

Design
Karen Wilks

Illustration
Kavel Rafferty
Silhouettes © 4D2A

Index
Christine Shaw

www.debretts.com

Guide to
ENTERTAINING
ETIQUETTE

Good Manners

Spring

Summer

Autumn

Winter

The Perfect Host

"At a dinner party one should eat wisely but not too well, and talk well but not too wisely." W SOMERSET MAUGHAM

Preface

There are a myriad ways in which you can entertain at home – from formal dinners, drinks parties and impromptu suppers to overnight stays, children's parties, al fresco lunches, summer picnics and barbecues. While these events may vary greatly in formality, scope and ambition, they are all united by one common feature, the host. The annual round of social events and rituals, which we all share and enjoy, is inevitably enhanced by faultless hospitality. As a host you must embody many contradictions; you will need to be both flexible and systematic, relaxed and decisive, impulsive and methodical. Above all, you must be generous: the simplest supper dish – if it is delicious, plentiful and accompanied by bountiful supplies of wine and good conversation – will be much more memorable than an artful arrangement of delicacies and very little bonhomie.

Approach the social dates in your diary with enthusiasm and liberality and, above all, remember that good manners will ensure that your guests feel cosseted and cared for. Good entertaining etiquette isn't about adhering to an outmoded and rigid code of conduct; it's about being aware of other people and doing your utmost to ensure that they are well looked after and having a wonderful time.

"Ask not what you can do for your country. Ask what's for lunch."
Orson Welles

"One cannot think well, love well, sleep well, if one has not eaten well."
Virginia Woolf

Good Manners

Being the perfect host requires an ability to plan ahead, excellent organisational skills and above all an ability to adapt to changing circumstances. Whether you're hosting a formal dinner, an ambitious drinks party or simply entertaining elderly relatives for the night or organising a kids' party, you have to accept that your best-laid plans may go awry. Try, whenever possible, to anticipate and pre-empt difficulties; you can find out about dietary regimes and allergies, lay in extra stores, have local taxi cab numbers to hand and ensure you've mollified the neighbours. But if the guests are drunk, the red wine is spilt on the carpet and you're beset by gatecrashers, your entertaining challenge is to remain positive, flexible and accommodating throughout.

Golden Rules for Good Hosts

Whatever you're planning, whether it is a
dinner party, drinks party or informal lunch,
you won't go wrong if you stick to these
basic golden rules.

Don't become a victim of vaunting ambition. Take a long,
hard look at your budget, culinary abilities and venue and
tailor your social occasion to fit your capabilities. If you go
for elaborate grandeur when space is limited and money is
tight, the event may fall flat.

Entertain within your comfort zone and don't bite off more than you can chew.

Make the nature of the event absolutely clear to your
guests. They will feel understandably annoyed if they turn
up at a formal dinner in jeans and trainers, and will leave
grumpy as well as hungry if they're expecting a buffet and
are only given canapés.

If you're sending real invitations, remember these will give
the guests clues about what to expect. So don't use a Comic
Sans typeface if you're planning formality, and remember
that conventional Copperplate will have most guests
reaching for their black tie.

Give guests as much information as possible about food, dress, venue and timings.

Remember that your primary role is to be the host/hostess.
You must be aware of all your guests all of the time, so
don't allow yourself to be waylaid into an intimate *tête à tête*,
while the other guests go hungry and thirsty.

Circulate and give your full attention to everyone you've invited.

Your job is to oil the wheels of conversations, make
introductions and ensure that no guest is feeling bored,
excluded or overwhelmed. Don't take this duty to a
ridiculous extreme – sweeping in and breaking up an
animated conversation to make a new introduction will
only cause irritation.

Observe your guests, and ensure that no-one is feeling like a wallflower.

REMEMBER THE GUEST IS KING

You must be infinitely accommodating of requirements, whims and foibles. Even if you feel intolerant of food fads and special diets you must do your best to cater for them (provided they have been communicated to you in advance). And every guest has a right to abstain from alcohol without argument.

If guests are demanding or fussy accept their behaviour with equanimity.

You must ensure that your guests have plenty to eat and drink – keep your eyes open at all times for empty glasses. Don't force drink or second helpings on refuseniks. However long the event lasts, you must stay the course. If you really don't want the evening to linger on into the small hours, you should warn your guests beforehand.

Stay until the bitter end – remember the evening is entirely your responsibility.

Entertaining Faux Pas

Blunders and misjudgements are an inevitable part of entertaining, and you have to accept that not every event will run smoothly. But with a little forethought and caution you should be able to avoid the most obvious mistakes.

CULTURAL AND RELIGIOUS CLASHES

Inviting guests who are practising Jews or Muslims and serving them your signature dish of suckling pig is a dietary *faux pas*. While nobody expects you to be *au fait* with all the finer aspects of food prohibitions, you should at least acknowledge your guests' religion and culture. The best policy is to ask them beforehand to let you know what they really can't eat and to accommodate these no-go areas in your menu planning.

ALLERGY ALERT

Seeing one of your guests go into anaphylactic shock because you forgot to check whether the cheese biscuits contained peanut traces is a social gaffe from which it is hard to recover. Obviously, a guest who is seriously allergic will alert you to the problem, but you must be absolutely rigorous in your screening of ingredients, especially if you blithely tell the allergic guest that the food is safe to eat.

FOOD POISONING

No host wants to see guests running from the table, retching and clutching their stomachs. Poisoning your guest is probably the worst *faux pas* of all. Take some simple precautions: cook meat well and, if you really want to play safe, avoid shellfish and molluscs – if there's just one bad one in the batch everybody's life will be a misery. Remember to cook joints of meat properly; never leave burgers pink.

Practise basic food hygiene measures: wipe down surfaces and chopping boards with an antiseptic spray, keep food refrigerated, adhere to freezing and defrosting guidelines, never serve food beyond its sell-by date.

FAUX PAS
Noun, plural faux pas
A slip or blunder in etiquette, manners, or
conduct; an embarrassing social blunder or
indiscretion.

Origin 1670–80, French
literally 'false step'

Synonyms
Error; impropriety

INADEQUATE SUPPLIES
Realising that you've run out of booze or butter halfway through the evening and making a quick dash to the
24-hour-supermarket is deeply discouraging. Your guests
will be irritated by your disorganisation and may even feel
insulted by your lack of forethought. Avoid this *faux pas* by
making comprehensive shopping lists before the event.

DRUNK AND DISORDERLY
Hosting an event can be stressful and it's tempting to enjoy
swigging the cooking wine as you stir your sauces. But it's
a real *faux pas* to get drunk before your guests arrive, and
scarcely preferable to lose the plot during the course of the
evening. It's your job to stay calm and in control.

As a host you're in charge of the event and your cooking
and entertaining will soon deteriorate if you hit the bottle.
If you don't want the evening to descend into anarchy,
drink moderately and alternate alcohol with water.

GUEST GAFFES
While you may not wish your evening's entertainment to
be bland and boring, it's risky to court controversy. So take
a long, hard look at your guest list beforehand.

Think carefully about inviting ex-partners, estranged
partners accompanied by their new love interest, people
who have fallen out in the past, people at opposite ends
of the political, cultural or religious spectrum. An ardent
atheist, paired with a crusading Christian, might get the
sparks flying, but it may take all your social skills to keep
the conflict light-hearted and entertaining.

DO UNTO OTHERS...
If your guests arrive at an informal supper in full evening
regalia, are horribly late and start swigging the lemon-
scented water in the finger bowls and eating the outer
leaves of the globe artichokes, what do you do? It's a
real *faux pas* to comment on other people's mistakes and
misjudgements. Gloss over their errors, don't make a fuss,
and if the occasion demands, embrace their errors yourself.

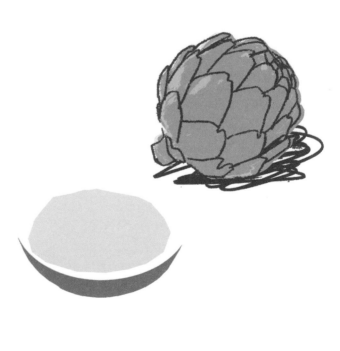

"Experience is the
name everyone gives
to their mistakes."
Oscar Wilde

Entertaining Dilemmas

No matter how organised you are and how much planning and preparation you put into home entertaining, you can never fully anticipate the complications, from food fads to gatecrashers, that the guests themselves will introduce. If you anticipate some of these issues you will be able to handle them with aplomb.

FOOD FETISHES

Hosting any social occasion involves, first and foremost, the challenge of providing food that all your guests will be able to eat. Not only do you have to cope with religious restrictions and various nuances of vegetarianism, but you may also have to accommodate a range of diets and regimes that exclude whole food groups.

If you are warned beforehand you must try to cope with all dietary requirements.

In an ideal world, all your guests will be omnivorous: if you find yourself at the head of a dinner party table confronted by a pescatarian, a vegetarian, a vegan, a guest who is lactose intolerant and someone with a peanut allergy, you have truly drawn the short straw. But there are always ways of accommodating multiple dietary requirements, even if it involves eschewing a main dish and opting for a mezze of mixed delicacies.

It's bad manners to tease, cajole or hector a guest about a 'supposed' food intolerance.

Your ability to cope with dietary mayhem is entirely dependent on being given adequate warning beforehand, and it is your guests' responsibility to do so. Guard against any last minute emergencies by ensuring that you always have supplies of non-controversial 'fillers': red lentils (it's easy to whip up a vegan dhal); hummus; bulghur (it will bulk up salad ingredients); brown rice; soy sauce.

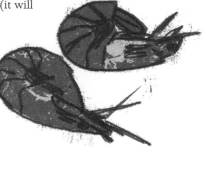
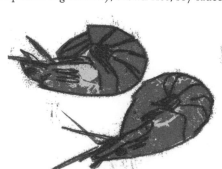

A GUIDE TO DIETARY REGIMES

VEGETARIAN: a diet that excludes meat. Vegetarians also avoid foods containing by-products of animal slaughter, such as animal-derived rennet and gelatin.

VEGAN: a type of vegetarian diet that excludes meat, eggs, dairy products and all other animal-derived ingredients.

PESCATARIAN: a diet that excludes all meat and animal flesh with the exception of fish.

MACROBIOTIC: a diet that excludes processed and refined foods, with an emphasis on whole grains, fruits and vegetables, and the occasional consumption of fish.

THE UNINVITED GUEST

Every host dreads the last minute phone call announcing the imminent arrival of the uninvited guest. Although the request may be inconvenient, you should always try and be accommodating – it's what being hospitable is all about.

If your carefully planned main course is going to have to be divided into ever smaller portions compensate by offering plenty of nibbles and/or *hors d'oeuvre*. Fill your store cupboard with nuts, olives, sun dried tomatoes and artichoke hearts and ensure you've always got plenty of parmesan cheese. With these supplies, and fresh bread (which can be bought at the last minute) you should be able to turn out an impressive range of bruschettas.

Don't seek to please a vegetarian at the expense of the carnivorous majority.

ALLERGY AWARE
The following foods are to blame for 90% of allergic reactions. If in doubt, they're best avoided:

Milk, eggs
Peanuts
Nuts from trees
(including Brazil nuts, hazelnuts, almonds and walnuts)
Fish, shellfish
Soya, wheat

Be gracious about last minute arrivals and hide all signs of panic and disarray.

Table Manners

The cause of much social anxiety, table manners are all too often associated with an arcane list of duties and proscriptions. Confronting your guests with a battery of cutlery and an array of glasses, in an attempt to 'dress up' your table, may well cause confusion and embarrassment.

GOLDEN RULES

Your napkin (avoid calling them serviettes) should be placed on your lap, never tucked it into your shirt. Dab the corners of your mouth if necessary during your meal, do not make grand wiping gestures. When you leave the table place your napkin, unfolded, beside your plate.

Sit up straight and make sure that your elbows don't encroach on your neighbour's space. Do not rest your elbows on the table or lean on them when eating.

If you are served a meal on the plate (rather than serving yourself), wait until everyone has been served before picking up your cutlery.

When dining in a group, do offer side dishes around the table, and hold them to assist your neighbour.

Don't reach across the table to grab serving dishes; politely ask for the dish to be passed to you.

Eat at a relaxed pace and don't wolf down course after course. Pace yourself to match your fellow diners.

Keep your mouth closed and noise to a minimum. Never smack your chops, or talk with your mouth full. Take care not to take mouthfuls that are too big.

Avoid talking while there is food in your mouth – even when you have a conversational gem up your sleeve.

When you have finished, place your knife and fork – with the tines facing upwards – together on your plate.

When faced with food that is not to your taste, soldier on to avoid hurt feelings and compliment the cook.

When using a fingerbowl, dip your fingers one hand at a time, rub gently to remove any stickiness and then dry them on your napkin.

CUTLERY ESSENTIALS

A knife should be held firmly in your right hand, with the handle tucked into your palm, your thumb down one side of the handle and your index finger along the top (but never touching the top of the blade).

You should never eat off a knife or hold it like a pencil.

When used with a knife or spoon, the fork should be held in the left hand, in much the same way as the knife, with the prongs facing downwards. On its own, it is held in the right hand, with the prongs facing upwards, resting on the fingers and secured with the thumb and index finger.

A spoon is held in the right hand, resting on the fingers and secured with the thumb and index finger. Food should be eaten off the side of the spoon – no slurping.

A spoon should never be used at a right angle to the mouth.

Cutlery should be rested on the plate/bowl between bites, and placed together in the bottom-centre when you are finished. Don't scrape your cutlery noisily against your plate or bowl. Equally, it is bad manners to loudly clank your utensils against your teeth.

Never gesture with your cutlery.

The range of a cutlery arsenal will depend on the formality of the occasion, but the layout should always be the same – fork to the left, knives and spoons to the right. Work from the outside inwards, course by course. Pudding implements sit above the place setting.

Always use cutlery, not fingers, in a formal setting.

You may eat chicken and pizza with your fingers if you are at a barbecue, finger buffet or very informal setting. Otherwise always use a knife and fork. It's fine to shell prawns with your fingers; use a fingerbowl if it is provided.

Challenging Foods

When is it acceptable to eat with your fingers? How do you dispose of bones and stones? Should oysters be slurped from the shell or pronged with a fork? The diverse range of foods that we eat can throw up many manners challenges. Remember, making a mistake only matters if you let your embarrassment get the better of you. On the other hand, eating with your mouth open and grabbing food from under other people's noses is genuinely offensive.

How to...
SQUEEZE A LEMON
You can either squeeze the lemon with your fingers, or against the tines of a fork, which channels the juice. It is polite to cup your hand around the lemon while squeezing so you don't spray those around you.

ASPARAGUS
Unless asparagus is a vegetable accompaniment to a dish, or covered in sauce, it should be eaten with the fingers. The asparagus spear should be picked up towards the end of the stem, dipped in any accompanying sauce and lowered into the mouth, bite by bite. Don't oversauce it or you'll have to contend with drips. There's no need to chew through the tough, woody ends of the stems; they should be left neatly on the side of the plate.

GLOBE ARTICHOKES
The leaves of an artichoke should be peeled off one by one, starting with the outer leaves. Hold each leaf by its pointy tip and dip the base in the butter or sauce. Eat just the tender, rounded base of each leaf, and leave the rest. Place discarded leaves on the side of the plate. When you reach the centre, the smaller leaves and hairy choke can be cut away to reveal the tender heart. This can be cut into pieces and eaten with a knife and fork.

"He was a bold man that first ate an oyster."
Jonathan Swift

LOBSTER

A whole lobster in its shell will typically arrive at your table already cut into two. It is fine to use just your fork while holding the shell steady with your hand.

The big claws usually come cracked but if not you will need to use special lobster crackers. Once you've cracked the claws pull out the meat with a fork. If you want to get meat out of the smaller attachments use a lobster pick. If you are daunted by the extrication process, opt for lobster thermidor; the white meat is extracted, cooked and then served in the shell.

WHOLE FISH

Work down one side of the spine at a time, from head-end to tail-end. Ease mouthful-sized pieces from the fish. Never flip the fish over to reach the flesh on the underside - lift the entire bone up and gently ease the flesh out from beneath. Small bones should be removed from the mouth with fingers and placed on the side of the plate. When in doubt, order a fillet. In some better restaurants the waiter will skilfully fillet the fish for you at the table.

PRAWNS

If your prawn arrives intact, begin by the removing head and tail; just give each end a sharp tug. Peel off the shell, starting from the underside where the legs meet the body. If your prawn is uncooperative, discreetly bend it against its natural curve to loosen the shell.

Finally, remove the black thread from along the back before devouring the flesh. If a prawn is served headless but with its tail attached, use the latter as a handle and discard after eating the flesh. Dip your fingers in a fingerbowl (if provided) and dry with a napkin.

MUSSELS

You can use an empty mussel shell as a pincer to extract the other mussels from their shells. Using a fork to ease out the mussels is also perfectly acceptable. The sauce around the mussels can be mopped up with pieces of bread or with a spoon. Put all empty shells on the spare plate provided and use the fingerbowl and napkin as required.

OYSTERS

Oysters are served already shucked (i.e. detached), but you can use your fork to prise the flesh from the shell. Squeeze the lemon over the oyster in the shell.

Pick up the shell and bring the widest end to your lips. Tilt, and slide the entire contents of the shell – the oyster and all the juices – directly into your mouth. Alternatively, you can hold the oyster in your left hand and spear the contents with a fork, then drink the juice from the shell.

You can chew the oyster, or swallow it down in one. If you chew you can savour its unique briny, metallic taste.

Formal Entertaining

Nowadays, we tend to opt for a relaxed and informal style of entertaining without the restraints of old-fashioned rules and rituals. However, every now and again there may be the need to organise a more formal, traditional dinner – for example if you are required to entertain a very grand guest…

'At Home' invitations are the best option for formal occasions; the most versatile style merely have 'At Home' and 'R.S.V.P.' engraved or printed on them. They would usually measure 5$\frac{1}{2}$ x 3$\frac{1}{2}$ inches (14 x 9 cm). The hostess then adds her name, address, date, time, names of guests and other necessary information by hand. They should be sent out about a month in advance; envelopes should always be handwritten (never typed) and stamps used (never franked).

The host should sit with the leading female guest to his right; the hostess should have the leading male guest to her right. Spouses of the principal guests sit to the left of the host and hostess. Couples are split and guests are alternated boy-girl as far as possible. Place cards should always be handwritten, and the names kept brief – honours, decorations, degrees, styles by office etc., are omitted – for example, Mr John Debrett. Titled guests are styled socially, e.g. Lord Debrett, rather than Earl of Debrett.

Invitations to formal events should be sent by post, never telephoned or emailed.

The Ten Rules of Conversation

1. *Strike a perfect balance between talking and listening.*
2. *Take an active interest in the other person.*
3. *Opt for some light humour, shared observation and gentle flattery.*
4. *The occasional well-placed compliment usually works wonders.*

Mr John Debrett

Pay attention to the little details when it comes to seating and serving.

Guests should arrive a few minutes late; the hosts should make introductions.

5. Ask questions, but don't conduct an aggressive interview.

6. Familiarity comes with time, so be aware of unspoken barriers.

7. Avoid strong opinion or stark honesty.

8. Remember that controversial views may offend.

9. Never talk about money, illness or death.

10. Don't bluff, lie, name-drop or brag.

Remember the hierarchy of introductions: men should be introduced to women, juniors to elder people and higher ranks. Introduce individuals to the group first and then the group to the individual. At formal events, it is polite (even if a little old-fashioned) to include surnames. If possible, offering a little information about each person as you introduce them ("John and I were at school together") will help to break the ice. The traditional British greeting on introduction is "How do you do?". The appropriate response – however strange it may seem – is to reiterate the phrase "How do you do?".

Food is always served from the left, and drink from the right. If communal serving dishes are used, they should be passed around the table in an anti-clockwise direction so that guests can serve their food from the left. Traditionally, the most important female guest should be served first, and then the rest of the table, going in a clockwise direction. Glasses should be filled as soon as guests are seated, and kept well topped-up for the duration of the meal. Gone are the days when women retired from the table before the men; coffee is usually served away from the table allowing guests to mix company again.

DRESS CODES

Dressing for a formal evening function at home is a tricky business. While a specific dress code should be stated on the invitation – for example 'black tie' – the frequently used catch-all phrase of 'come as you are' can leave guests in a quandary. If invitations are sent by post, then it is safe to assume that the evening will be relatively formal, so the men should wear jackets and women should look smart.

"What ho!" I said.
"What ho!" said Motty.
"What ho! What ho!"
"What ho! What ho! What ho!"
After that it seemed rather difficult
to go on with the conversation.
Jeeves and the Unbidden Guest, P.G. Wodehouse

Dinner Parties

The more carefully you plan a dinner party –
from the guest list and table arrangements to
the menu and timings – the more likely it is
to succeed. Remember, being a good host is
hard work.

FORMAL OR INFORMAL?

Decide at the outset just how formal or informal you want
your dinner party to be. For a relaxed and casual evening
you might opt for a main course that guests can serve
themselves from serving dishes on the table. Starters may
be as simple as bread and olives, with fruit and cheese for
pudding.

Food, table, decor and dress must all fit the formality of the occasion.

If you are aiming for a more formal evening, food should
be elegantly plated up in the kitchen (only do this if you're
confident of your presentation skills). Care should be taken
over starters and puddings as well as the main course.

POLISH

{ "A host is like a general:
calamities often
reveal his genius."
Horace }

A Well-Organised Evening

PREPARATION

Do as much as you can before the guests arrive. Lay the table, sort out the crockery, prepare as much food as possible – you will be able to spend more time with your guests rather than in the kitchen.

Spruce up the house and remove clutter. Ensure that there are clean towels and fresh soap in the cloakroom. Clear pegs for guests' coats, or designate a place where you will stow them away.

Make sure you have plenty of serving dishes and spoons. Fill the salt cellar and pepper mill.

Leave yourself plenty of time before the guests arrive to do the flower arrangements and add any finishing touches to your table decorations.

Make sure you have some time for yourself. Indulge in a relaxing bath and take your time over getting dressed up – it's all part of the anticipation, and will get you in the mood for the evening ahead.

PLANNING

Time spent carefully planning the menu will be invaluable and will ensure that your evening runs smoothly.

Think of all the courses and try to keep your menu balanced. If you're serving a hearty main course keep the starter and pudding light.

Aim to please: remember that not everyone will appreciate mind-blowing spice or nose-to-tail eating.

Don't experiment: go for tried and tested recipes. Remember that sometimes the simplest dishes, perfectly executed and utilising the best ingredients, are the biggest crowd-pleasers.

Quality is better than quantity. Just a couple of well-made side dishes are preferable to a huge range of under/overcooked vegetables.

Set off your meal with the best bread available and homemade dressings and sauces. A well-stocked cheeseboard will always impress – add special biscuits and chutneys.

WELCOMING GUESTS

Create an inviting ambience for guests – subtle lights, gentle background music, nuts and olives already set out in bowls.

Take your guests' coats and settle them into their seats before offering them drinks. Don't leave guests nervously holding their coats in the kitchen, waiting for a drink, while you are preoccupied with the cooking.

If you are entertaining as a couple, employ some teamwork. For example, one of you cooks and serves, the other gets drinks and clears the table. Ensure you don't leave guests on their own for long periods while you clatter around in the kitchen.

When it's time to seat guests at the table, make sure you have a plan. If you don't mind a free-for-all, just invite guests to seat themselves.

However, if you have an informal seating plan in your mind, explain clearly to guests where you want them to sit. You might have even created a formal seating plan – according to genders, age and interests – and used handwritten place cards to indicate where guests should sit.

SCHEDULING

Work out your timings:

🕐 Drinks: don't let the drinks drag on too long – an hour to an hour-and-a-half is enough time for everyone to settle and have one or two aperitifs. Serve some canapés to ensure that guests aren't drinking on empty stomachs.

🕐 Ensure that the food is ready when you call everyone to the table. Starters should be on the table (or about to be), and the main course should be on hold, ready to serve up.

🕐 It's acceptable to clear away starter plates promptly but allow guests to linger over their main course, especially if there are seconds to be had.

🕐 Don't rush people and don't completely clear the table while they're still sitting there. Just remove the dirty dishes.

🕐 Invite people to leave the table for coffee and liqueurs – the move away from the table signals that the evening is entering its closing stages.

🕐 If it's all going on too long, deploy subtle hints – cups of coffee, offers of taxi numbers or spare beds.

Impromptu Entertaining

Every now and again we can find ourselves with some unexpected hungry guests to feed. It might be an spur-of-the-moment visit from relatives, a last minute invitation to friends, or simply drinks that turn into supper… Whatever the situation, it is important to have a few tricks up your sleeve and a few supplies in the cupboard so you can throw together an impromptu meal.

ATTITUDE COUNTS

An impromptu lunch or supper requires your best 'can do' attitude. Even if you're mentally scouring the cupboards in a blind panic as to what you can serve up, never let on to your guests. The charming host is always capable and calm (on the outside).

TIME IS OF THE ESSENCE

A last minute supper is not the time to disappear into the kitchen for hours on end to attempt a gastronomic dinner. Keep it quick, easy and well within your culinary capabilities. Aim to have something delicious and digestible in front of your guests promptly.

PERFECT SETTINGS

Don't be tempted to dig out your best china, polish your finest crystal and buff up the heirloom silver. Instead, lay up the kitchen table and create a cosy, jovial and relaxed atmosphere. It will also save you minutes when you're serving up, and allow you to maximize your time with your unexpected guests.

ATTENTION TO DETAIL

Dress up your setting with a few little details: a tablecloth and napkins, a few tea lights or candles, and some background music. Keep your guests' glasses topped-up and put out some bowls of nibbles. Before you know it, you will have created a hospitable ambience and your impromptu supper will have turned into a social event.

Quick Pastas

Puttanesca:
garlic, chilli, olive oil, anchovy fillets, tinned tomatoes, black olives, capers, spaghetti.

Pesto:
pine nuts, parmesan, garlic, olive oil, fresh basil, pasta.

Carbonara:
olive oil, garlic, pancetta, eggs, parmesan.

EASY EGGS
Spanish tortilla: onion, potatoes, olive oil, eggs.
Cheese omelette: eggs, butter, cheese.
Poached eggs: eggs, butter, toast.

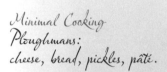

Minimal Cooking
Ploughmans:
cheese, bread, pickles, pâté.

Salad Niçoise:
tuna, green beans, black olives,
eggs, tomatoes, lettuce.

Gazpacho:
tomatoes, cucumber, bread,
garlic, sherry vinegar, olive
oil.

TAKEAWAY ETIQUETTE
If you really are in a position where you can't muster up a meal, then call for a takeaway. Never try to pass it off as your own cooking, so come clean with your guests. Make an occasion of it, allowing your guests to name their cuisine of choice.

Takeaways should be eaten off warmed plates, and decanted into suitable china serving dishes. Where possible, try to make the meal as authentic as you can – for example, dig out some chopsticks and serve suitable accompaniments (soy sauce, mango chutney, lime pickle etc.).

It goes without saying that the host should foot the bill and tip the delivery person. Equally, guests should always write a note or send an email to their hosts to thank them, even though the evening was very informal...

"A crust eaten in peace is better than a banquet partaken in anxiety."
Aesop

Drinks Parties

The party scene is packed with countless variables. No two gatherings are ever the same, and even with an identical venue, refreshments and music, no party can ever be recreated. Atmosphere is an elusive commodity, and it falls on the shoulders of the host to create the right conditions for bonhomie to flourish.

Make it clear if you're serving food – buffet, canapés, light supper etc.

GET THE MOOD RIGHT...

Dress up your rooms with striking flower arrangements and pay careful attention to the lighting. Use lamps and fairy lights, or light candles – but make sure they're safely tucked away.

Your party may turn into a wild bacchanalia, but certainly at the start music (if used) should be subtle and non-challenging. If possible, create 'quiet rooms' away from the maelstrom, where guests can withdraw for conversation.

Five Steps to Hosting a Perfect Drinks Party

THE GUEST LIST

Don't focus on a single group or clique – introduce new blood. Invite friends from different social circles, and ask them to bring friends or partners. Ensure that everyone at your party will be given the chance to meet someone new.

THE INVITATION

Make the nature of the event absolutely clear in the invitation. If you're just ringing around or emailing, people will assume the event is informal. If you're sending out printed invitations, pay special attention to the design and typography. It would be unforgivably pretentious, and actually very misleading, to issue a formal invitation to a party where guests will be bringing their own bottles, basic food is served straight from the oven, and dancing is to your own CDs.

Don't leave anything to chance – if you have a specific dress code in mind, state it clearly on the invitation (even if it's just a general directive).

Make it clear what type of food you're going to be serving. You can specify an end time if you don't want the event to drag on.

THE DRINK

Make sure that your bar (or drinks table) is in an easily accessible location. You don't want a frantic bottle-neck, with guests trying desperately to reach the booze.

If you're using serving staff (or even your kids and their teenage friends) make sure you brief them clearly before the event and that they are instructed to never leave a glass empty…

Calculate (generously) how much alcohol per head and over-supply. A party that runs dry is an irredeemable social failure.

If possible, keep stocks of white wine, sparkling wine and champagne chilled in the fridge; if there's no room use ice buckets generously packed with crushed ice (buy it in bags beforehand).

Provide interesting non-alcoholic alternatives: elderflower cordial, ginger beer, fruit cup. Guests who are abstaining shouldn't be condemned to a bread and water diet.

THE FOOD

It's irresponsible to ply people with alcohol without supplying food. At its most basic this can be crisps, nuts, olives, and booze-absorbing hunks of bread and cheese/ham.

More sophisticated catering can range from exquisite canapés to cooked sausages, chicken wings and meatballs, or a buffet supper of cold ham, chicken, salmon and salads.

Remember, however, that this is primarily a drinks party. The more ambitious your catering the more provision you will have to make. Buffets or hot food will require plates, cutlery and space in which your guests can serve themselves and eat in comfort. If you're entertaining a large number of people in your home this might be overwhelming. Think carefully and plan your catering realistically.

If you're offering canapés these must be handed round to guests. For a big affair, it's worth employing some respectable teenagers, or – if your children are old enough – asking them to help. If you don't have hired help you will certainly need to make it a designated duty.

THE HOST

You're responsible for the party from beginning to end, and that means staying reasonably sober. You will need to have your wits about you, so that you can observe the comings and goings of your guests.

Watch out for wallflowers; if certain guests are finding it hard to mingle, it's your job to swoop in, make introductions and indulge in social engineering.

Keep your eye on supplies; monitor drink and food and ensure that both are flowing.

Take the time to do some subtle housekeeping; clear away discarded glasses, half-eaten plates of food and brimming ashtrays throughout the evening. You don't want things to get too squalid.

Monitor noise levels; remember your neighbours and don't let your guests take control of the volume knob. You don't want irate confrontations on your front doorstep.

Stay up until the bitter end. Send stragglers home in taxis, arrange beds for non-movers. Turns the lights out and the music off. The party's over…

Drinks Parties Dilemmas

Hosting a drinks party can be a hazardous affair. Your guests may not behave according to your script, and you might find that you're forced to deal with rowdy behaviour, gatecrashers and outraged neighbours. Plan ahead and you should be able to negotiate these dilemmas with a cool head.

THE DRUNK GUEST

If you're a liberal host and the drink flows freely at your parties, you will have to accept that you're running the risk of acquiring some guests who are well over the limit.

Always have a list of taxi and mini-cab numbers close at hand.

Observe signs of impending drunkenness carefully. Don't intervene in a heavy-handed way ("I think you've had enough"). Just steer the guest to a quiet corner and attempt to ply him/her with some strong black coffee and stodgy food. You might even suggest that they lie down for an hour or two.

If your guest has reached the stage of maudlin introspection, verbal (or even physical) aggression, or neediness and over-emotionalism, the fun is really over. Take executive action and order a taxi. When it arrives announce decisively "Oh look, your taxi's arrived".

Ignore any protests from the guests about not having ordered the taxi, just propel them firmly towards it. If they're drunk enough, they may even assume that they're suffering from a momentary memory lapse.

Don't berate drunk guests while they're still intoxicated — they won't remember.

If you've got a belligerent drunk who's insisting on driving home, you may have to resort to desperate measures, e.g. hiding coats and car keys, blocking their car in, or even – as a last resort – plying him/her with an incredibly strong, unconsciousness-inducing 'last drink'. It's better to have a drunk guest sleeping it off on your sofa than to hear news of a terrible accident the following morning.

Specify on invitations whether your guests can bring friends/partners.

THE GATECRASHER

If you identify a guest who is a gatecrasher, ask around and make sure that none of your other guests know who they are before taking any steps. A guest may have brought a friend without clearing it with you – this is inconsiderate, but you'll have to live with it.

If your uninvited guest has no party connections, you should approach him/her and explain that this is an invitation-only party. Ask them politely if they have perhaps made a mistake and are looking for another location? This normally causes embarrassment and instant retreat.

If your gatecrasher decides to brazen it out, you must decide whether you're prepared to accept the intrusion (perhaps they look interesting or amusing – but this is a risky strategy). If not, you should ask them, firmly and politely, to leave. A repeated refusal to do so means that you will have to call the police, and you should make it clear to your gatecrasher that you're prepared to do so.

THE OUTRAGED NEIGHBOUR

It is absolutely essential that you warn your neighbours when you are planning a party. Do so a few days before the date, just in case they want to make escape plans. Whenever possible, invite neighbours along – it's much harder to feel outraged when you're on the inside looking out.

Before the party begins, make a decision about a reasonable time to quieten down. Remember that after midnight, many neighbours will feel justified in complaining, so it might be a good idea to stop playing loud music soon after twelve. Once you've made your decision, tell your guests about it and stick to it.

If guests stay on into the early hours, try and ensure that goodbyes and final chats take place within your house – not in the drive or on the street. Remind guests that it's late and you don't want to disturb the neighbours. If a neighbour comes round to complain, listen politely, apologise and turn down the music.

It's quite acceptable to specify a finishing time on your invitation.

When It All Goes Wrong…

Despite your best-laid plans you will inevitably experience accidents, disappointments and failures when you are entertaining. It's important not to panic, to keep calm, and to realise that there are very few kitchen emergencies that can't be handled as long as you've got a well-stocked storecupboard and freezer.

OVERSEASONING

Seasoning is a delicate art and, in the rush to get a dish ready for the table, it's all too easy to overdo it. Don't despair, there are a number of tried and tested remedies…

DILUTION Soups and stews that are overseasoned can be rescued by dilution. Add water, in small increments, and taste as you do so.

ADDITION Add more vegetables, grains or noodles to soups and stews – they will soak up the extra salt/pepper.

THE POTATO TRICK Cut up a raw potato in chunks and add it to a soup or stew. It will act as a sponge, absorbing the salt. Leave the potato chunks to do their magic work for a few minutes, then remove and discard them.

OVER SPICY? If your dish is flaming hot, add some sugar or honey to adjust the seasoning.

COOL DOWN Dairy products will offset the painful side-effects of over-spicy food. Serve hot curries and salsas with a side dish of yoghurt (a cucumber raita for instance) or sour cream (add chives).

SICKLY SWEET If you've overdone the sugar and honey, you can offset the sweetness with the addition of citrus juice, wine or vinegar.

Spills and Breakages

If you're plying guests with alcohol you run the risk of spills and breakages. As a host it's your job to quell any post-accident furore and put a lid on the culprit's self-reproach. There are few stains that can't be removed…

If a guest damages something that is obviously valuable, they should offer to compensate you, and you should (within reason) politely refuse.

Red Wine Remedies
A little white wine will neutralise the effect that the red wine will have on your carpet. If the stain has dried, dab it with soda water. The carbonation in the soda helps to lift the colour from the carpet fibres. Salt will keep the stain from setting in. Leave it on the carpet for about 30 minutes before vacuuming it up.
Alternatively, mix two parts hydrogen peroxide and one part washing-up liquid and use a sponge to dab the stain gently.

WHAT'S THAT SMELL?
If your guests are arriving any minute and you've just burnt the main course you'll need to get rid of that ominous smell. Open all the doors and windows to air the house. Try simmering a couple of cinnamon sticks in a saucepan of water, or burning scented candles. Air freshener won't mask the smell; it will just suffuse your house with a chemical stink.

EMERGENCY REMEDY
If you've burnt the main course or up-ended the roasting pan on the kitchen floor you'll need some back-up.

Stock your freezer with emergency supplies. Chicken breast fillets will grill super-quickly (you can use the microwave, or a jug of hot water, to defrost them). You can dress them up with a mushroom sauce, drizzle pesto (a store-cupboard stalwart) over them, or whip up a quick tomato, olive oil and garlic sauce and serve with parmesan.

BULK IT UP
Rice, French bread, peas from the freezer and salad can all be used to make your table look as if it's groaning with food. Always ensure you've got some decent cheese, and you can add a cheese course at the last minute.

HAS YOUR CHEESECAKE GONE GLOOPY?
Most pudding disasters can be remedied by smothering the mistakes under a generous layer of fresh fruit. Depending on the season, strawberries, blackberries, or cranberries can all be deployed; if you're desperate even dried fruits – such as figs, raisins and dates – will do. Add lashings of cream or ice cream and your guests will be happy.

NEVER APOLOGISE, NEVER EXPLAIN
Remember, your guests don't know what you've planned to serve, so they won't be disappointed when it doesn't materialise. The main thing is to keep calm and reserve panic, rage and hysteria for the kitchen, with the door firmly closed. Present your emergency, or salvaged, dishes with confidence and aplomb and never go in for an apologetic commentary: "I'm so sorry, this was mean to be a fluffy soufflé, but it's as flat as a pancake…" etc., etc.

Entertaining Overnight Guests

Plan ahead to ensure that your guests have a truly enjoyable stay. Do everything you can to make the guest room comfortable, lay in stocks of suitable food and drink, think about outings and expeditions. Always accept offers of help, and don't turn yourself into a skivvy – that way you'll ensure both your guests and yourself enjoy the visit.

THE GUEST ROOM

Give your guest room a thorough spring clean and clear any clutter. Check that light bulbs are working and that windows can still be opened.

Make up the bed shortly before guests arrive – even clean sheets can smell stale if they're left on a bed for weeks. Provide plenty of pillows and extra blankets or quilts.

Leave a selection of reading material on the bedside table: magazines and books of short stories are ideal for a short stay. If possible, add something about your home town/village etc. – a guide to local history, a selection of local walks, an anthology of local poems.

Your guests might appreciate an alarm clock and, if you can spare one, a radio. Ensure that a bottle of mineral water and glasses are also supplied.

A vase of flowers on the bedside table or dressing-table is a good finishing-touch.

Ensure that you have provided your guest with plenty of clothes hangers and hanging space, as well as at least one empty drawer.

Provide plenty of clean, fluffy towels. Either leave them on the bed or, if the guests have their own bathroom, put them there.

Leave a basket of basic toiletries – soap, toothpaste, hand cream, body lotion, shampoo – in the bedroom. It's a good idea to amass these complimentary items when you stay in hotels, and your guests will really appreciate your care and attention to detail.

Golden Rules for Entertaining Overnight Guests

Check with your guests beforehand to make sure that they eat everything. If they plead serious allergies or intolerances, take the information seriously and accommodate them.

If guests are bringing young children, establish what they like to eat beforehand. Check if their parents proscribe certain foods or drinks – they will look askance if you're plying their kids with forbidden fizzy drinks and crisps.

Make sure guests are informed about any plumbing irregularities or restrictions – if the hot water is in short supply at certain times of the day they should be told.

Show guests where they can hang coats and deposit muddy boots.

Give guests plenty of space; they may want to spend time relaxing on their own.

Leave basic breakfast supplies in the kitchen before you go to bed – your guests might be early risers and you don't want them to go hungry.

Try not to make too big a deal about the meals you're having to cook. Your guests will feel very unrelaxed if you're flapping around the kitchen in a frenzy of noisy preparation. Don't be a martyr, accept offers of help if you feel you need a break.

If it's all getting a bit much, suggest a trip to the local pub. Most guests will enjoy the local colour, and it will give you some respite.

Suggest possible outings and expeditions (the guests will probably accede) but don't present them with a military-style programme of activities. Try not to be too managerial; your guests may have their own plans and preferences.

Even if you only drink herbal teas and think caffeine is the work of the devil, you must make sure that you have adequate supplies of tea and coffee in the house.

Ensure that you have offered your guests a drink or refreshment within living memory. Don't let them sit empty-handed and thirsty because you've forgotten to make a cup of tea or pour a glass of wine.

The Perfect Breakfast

You may be a tea or a coffee person, a fan of the fry-up or prefer something light – everyone has different tastes when it comes to breakfast. It is, however, an important meal and one which, done well, can be an appetising and sociable start to the day.

MORNING MANNERS

Breakfast can be a difficult time, especially if not everyone around the table is a 'morning person'. If you are blessed with a constitution that gives you an enthusiasm for the morning, then approach breakfast with caution and read the mood before inflicting your sunny disposition on your companions. Respect the slower, quieter and more relaxed pace that is often preferred first thing, and allow everyone a cup of something in peace. Conversely, no matter how tired, unrested or apprehensive you feel about the day ahead, it is equally bad manners to bring a bad morning mood to the table.

WHY BREAKFAST MATTERS

During the night, your body regenerates itself by using the building materials from the food you ate the previous day; you also use about one litre of water through just breathing and sweating. Breakfast is, therefore, essential for restoring energy, replenishing building materials, rehydrating and maintaining blood sugar levels for consistent energy throughout the day. If you skip breakfast you're also likely to over-eat at lunchtime, or even snack at mid-morning, and you might find yourself putting on weight.

HOUSE GUESTS

It is wise to have a selection of breakfast options available if you have people staying. Tea and toast will do for most, but there is something extremely comforting about a cooked breakfast, especially on the weekend. But remember, if you're planning a substantial lunch a full fry-up might be too ambitious. Give your guests a rough idea of what time you usually take breakfast – there is nothing more embarrassing than hearing activity in the kitchen if you're still in bed. Guests and hosts should get dressed before going down to breakfast – save slopping about in your pyjamas for when you're home alone or en famille.

THE DETAILS

A successful breakfast is usually down to the details. Freshly brewed coffee and a large pot of tea are musts, along with a good selection of jams and spreads. Fresh juice should be readily available, and a well-stocked fruit bowl and a selection of pastries are also a welcome addition. If you are going to cook, then eggs and bacon are the starting blocks unless, of course, you choose to keep it simple with a decent bacon sandwich. A couple of newspapers should also be to hand.

> "'When you wake up in the morning, Pooh,' said Piglet at last,
> 'what's the first thing you say to yourself?'
> 'What's for breakfast?' said Pooh. 'What do you say, Piglet?'
> 'I say, I wonder what's going to happen exciting today?' said Piglet.
> Pooh nodded thoughtfully. 'It's the same thing,' he said."
>
> The House at Pooh Corner, A. A. Milne

The 10.30am Full English Breakfast

INGREDIENTS

Serves 2

4 top-quality pork sausages
4 rashers of dry-cure back bacon
2 slices of English black pudding
2 field mushrooms
1 can of baked beans
1 tomato, halved
2 eggs
2 slices bread
Vegetable oil
Butter
Salt and pepper
Sauce of choice
(tomato ketchup, brown sauce,
English mustard, etc.)

METHOD

10:00 Set the oven very low (about 100°C), turn the grill to high and put a large frying pan over a low-to-medium heat. Put two plates in the oven. Gather the ingredients.

10:05 Add the sausages and a dash of oil to the pan. Quarter-turn every few minutes.

10:10 Put the baked beans in a saucepan over a low heat. Stir occasionally.

10:15 Season the tomato and mushrooms with salt and pepper, and top with a knob of butter. Place under the hot grill. Add the bacon to the pan.

10:20 Divide the evenly-browned sausages between the plates in the oven. Turn the bacon and add black pudding. Turn the pudding after three minutes.

10:25 Divide the mushrooms, tomato, bacon and black pudding equally between plates in the oven. Toast the bread. Wipe out the pan with some kitchen roll, add a fresh splash of oil and crack in the eggs.

10:30 Remove the plates from the oven and add the baked beans and fried eggs. Butter the toast, cut in half and add to the side of the plate. Serve with preferred sauce.

Guest Dilemmas

No matter how much time you devote to planning overnight visits, there will also be pitfalls and problems that threaten to derail the stay. Most of these issues can be avoided by a pre-emptive strike: think ahead, alert guests to any potential difficulties and don't allow yourself to become frazzled.

Never berate your guests for their smoking habit or implore them to give up.

SMOKING

It's your home and your house rules apply. So if you're a non-smoker, who can't tolerate the smell of smoke, you aren't compelled to put up with your guests' smoking.

Decide what your policy is going to be, stick to it and make it absolutely clear to your guests. If at all possible, warn smoking guests that yours is a non-smoking household. Use a light touch: "I hope you won't mind being consigned to smoking on the patio", rather than a heavy-duty command: "We don't allow smoking in the house".

Do your best to make smokers feel comfortable. Create a cosy smoking area on the terrace or in the porch, with chairs, a table and a capacious ashtray.

OVERSTAYERS

The true houseguest from hell is that one that doesn't know when to leave. Pre-empt this problem by confirming arrival and departure times before the visit even begins. You can indicate, in the nicest possible way, that you have commitments: "Friday to Sunday will be ideal – I've got to go up to London for a meeting first thing Monday…" If you're saddled with an overstayer, bite the bullet and explain that all good things must come to an end…

CHILDREN

If you have young children and are expecting childless guests, make a few adjustments. Clear away as much of the child-related clutter as possible (you don't want your guests to break their necks tripping on errant pieces of Lego). Keep a close eye on your children and their interactions with your guests: if they're getting a little too strident, hyperactive or demanding, intervene. Finally, ensure that your children don't barge into your guests' bedroom demanding to play at 6am. Try your best to keep the house peaceful until a slightly more civilised hour.

If guests are bringing children, do your best to child-proof your house, stowing away fragile items and blocking stairways. Provide suitable food and drink, and dig out some board games, packs of cards and DVDs, just in case. You could mention to your guests beforehand that they might need to bring some extra entertainment for the kids.

However, it is difficult for you to reproach other people's children for their behaviour. So if they're charging up and down your landing at the crack of dawn, or insisting on staying up and disrupting your dinner at 11pm, you'll need to alert the parents. This can be done tactfully. For example, you could say that you've left out some breakfast cereals and a couple of DVDs just in case the kids wake up really early. Or you could tell your guests that you're planning to serve dinner at 8pm, which will give them time to bath the children and get them to bed beforehand. They really should get the message.

Don't allow the visit to be dominated and disrupted by your guests' children.

Pet Preoccupations

If you're a pet-owner you will inevitably become accustomed to the anti-social behaviour of your pets. You will be blissfully oblivious to the relentlessly squeaking hamster-wheel, the pungent smell of freshly-opened cat food, the dawn barking ritual, or the dog and cat hairs that strew your cushions and stick, glue-like, to guests' clothes.

But you really must think carefully about all these manifestations before inviting people to your home. You cannot simply assume that your friends and relations will share your tolerance and – within reason – you should do your best to accommodate their reservations (e.g. open the cat food when the guests are out of the room, vacuum your sofa before the guests arrive, oil the hamster-wheel etc.).

Check with your guests first; if your visitors are hesitant about animals or confess to an allergy to cat hair, don't inflict your animals upon them. Insouciantly exclaiming "she really likes you" as your feline-hating visitor flinches from the insistent kneading of a sharp-clawed cat, simply won't do.

If your guests are bringing dogs to an animal-free zone you should expect the same degree of consideration. If you're not much of a dog-lover, say so at the outset, and firmly mark out the boundaries before your guests arrive; e.g. say you're happy for the dog to stay in the kitchen/utility room, but you'd prefer it if it didn't colonise the sitting room/bedrooms.

Keep all pets out of guests' bedrooms, unless enthusiastically requested to do otherwise.

"Guests, like fish, begin to smell after three days."
Benjamin Franklin

Entertaining Elderly People

Whether you are hosting in-laws, grandparents or elderly friends or relatives, it is essential that you play the generation game. Even middle-aged guests will find their energy levels and priorities challenged by a household with young children, so you must think carefully about your guests' age, tastes, energies and disposition before inviting them to your home.

CREATE A COMFORTABLE ENVIRONMENT

Before welcoming elderly guests, examine your house carefully and make sure you're prepared.

Are there plenty of comfortable chairs? It can be difficult for elderly people to manoeuvre themselves out of very low-slung chairs and sofas. It's better to supply more upright chairs, with arm-rests (for leverage) and plenty of scatter cushions (for back support)

Have you supplied occasional tables? Some elderly people will find it hard to reach drinks that are on the floor, and won't want to juggle plates, cups and glasses on their laps. Provide handy tables adjacent to their chairs.

Is there enough light? Very dim lighting will play havoc with failing eyesight. Ensure that stairs, hallways and landings are well lit. Supply plentiful table lamps and bedside lamps, and opt for high-wattage bulbs.

Is your house warm enough? Older people are more liable to feel the cold, so turn up the thermostat, make sure doors remain closed and don't seat your guests in direct drafts.

Is your bathroom hazardous? Ensure that your guests are safe in the bathroom by placing anti-slip mats in the bath/shower. Check that bath-mats or rugs outside the bath/shower area have non-slip backing.

Is the floor area clear? You don't want your guests to trip and fall on a rogue toy – so check carefully that any potential hazards are stowed away.

MIND YOUR MANNERS

Never make the crass assumption that old age is inevitably partnered with senility. Talking to older people as if they're confused infants is the height of bad manners.

Never assume that older people are deaf as posts. True, some older people are hard of hearing and, if that is the case, it will become immediately apparent. It is unforgivably rude to shout at an older person as if he or she is an imbecile.

Different times, different manners. It is probably safe – unless you are instructed to the contrary – to assume that the older generation expects slightly more reticent and formal manners. This means taking the conversation at a slower pace, censoring off-colour jokes and stories, not swearing, and being respectful of, for example, religion (which might play an important role in your guest's life).

Be patient. Everybody slows down as they get older and everyday tasks (walking, eating, getting dressed, etc.) will inevitably take longer. Accept this with good grace.

Creating a Welcoming Atmosphere

AMEND YOUR TIMETABLE: Older guests will probably not want to eat an enormous dinner at 9pm. You may well find that they prefer a regular succession of small meals throughout the day. Adjust your usual timings to accommodate these requirements.

GIVE YOUR GUESTS PLENTY OF SPACE: Older guests may enjoy spending time in their own bedroom, or just sitting quietly in a comfortable chair away from the rest of the family. Don't try and provide too much stimulus – ensure that your guests have time to read, do crossword puzzles and watch the television.

KEEP AN EYE ON THE CHILDREN: Even if they're seeing their own grandchildren, you have to accept that most older people are a little less tolerant of the noise, disruption and havoc that children can create. So observe your kids and their interactions and, if you see any signs of incipient weariness or impatience, intervene and give your older guests a break.

DON'T OVERDO IT: Planning a packed timetable of country walks, stately home visits and pub lunches is laudable, but it's probably unrealistic. Try and pace the days, so that – for example – a morning outing is offset by a quiet afternoon of gentle chat and TV-viewing.

KEEP THE KETTLE ON: You may well find that older guests are very appreciative of regular cups of tea and biscuits throughout the day. They may be reticent about asking or 'being a nuisance' so remember to keep offering.

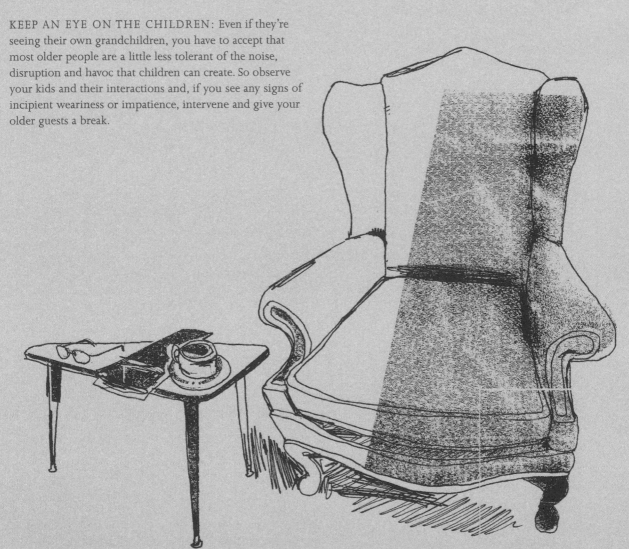

Children's Parties

The children's party is all too often the arena in which parental competition reaches its apotheosis, a red-blooded battle to outdo and trump each other, which can turn very nasty. A party at home, if it is well-organised and planned, may be much more successful that an expensive outing or trip to a commercial venue.

Entertaining children at home is comparatively inexpensive; it also allows you have more control over the proceedings and even to bring some creativity to the plans. Ideally, you will have a dedicated space (an attic, basement, playroom) that will accommodate the children comfortably, or you might want to think about using the garden (bad news for kids with winter birthdays).

Think carefully about the impact that excited children will have on your décor.

Most children will be absolutely thrilled by a diet of mini-sausages, burgers, chicken nuggets, white bread, cakes, biscuits and mini-chocolate bars, all washed down with lashings of fizzy drinks. If this junk food banquet sticks in your gorge, you can cook a more healthy and interesting menu at home. But be prepared for tantrums, rejections and refusals. Some of the party-goers may well find your homemade bread and hand-crafted meatballs inedible and – unlike adult guests – will make this perfectly clear.

Remove any valuable or fragile items and use old sheets to protect soft furnishings.

If you want to avoid a gang of hyper-excited kids running riot and trashing your home, you will need to think about formal entertainment. This could be as simple as organising some traditional party games (pass the parcel, pin the tail on the donkey, musical chairs, treasure hunt) etc.

Check allergies and food intolerances with mums beforehand and take them seriously.

Alternatively, you might want to hire a children's entertainer. Options include magicians and clowns, or maybe something novel, like a snake expert who comes round armed with an array of repulsive reptiles and allows the kids to handle them (this may end in tears if you have any phobics amongst your guests). The other option is to hire a piece of equipment – a bouncy castle, or a giant trampoline – which can be erected in your garden.

Entertaining Children

Party Games

Duck, Duck, Goose
Chinese Whispers
Find the Ticking Clock
Pin the Tail on the
* Donkey*
Desert Islands
Squeak, Piggy,
* Squeak*
Pass the Parcel

Children's parties are demanding social occasions. Not only do you have to cope with unpredictable guests, but you may also have to deal with competitive and uncooperative parents. Bite the bullet and remember that birthdays come round just once a year.

THE INVITATION

Send out proper invitations, don't rely on word-of-mouth. This doesn't need to be expensive; you can buy ready-made invitations to kids' parties (with blanks you fill in). Or you can have fun designing your own invitations on the PC – perhaps including a photograph or some wacky typography.

When your children are young it's best not to entrust the invitations to their care. All too often you'll find a bundle of battered envelopes at the bottom of their school bag just days before the party. A better option is to hand out the invitations yourself at the school gates.

Get your children to help you with handmade invitations.

You will want to have a good idea of the number of children involved. You should therefore put RSVP on your invitations.

If you are organising a party and find that you are suffering from a distinct lack of replies as the big day approaches, you have no alternative but to ring round, or track down the errant parents at the school gate.

You are invited to
Luke's Party
on Saturday
from 4–6pm

RSVP

THE PARTY BAG

Party bags were originally just cheap and cheerful receptacles for a slice of birthday cake and a novelty item or two. They have rapidly evolved into status items, packed to the brim with small toys. They have become very costly, and there is a risk of escalation as parents strive to 'keep up with the Joneses'. You can restore sanity by taking some very simple steps…

Set an upper price limit for party bags and stick to it. If you are working within a budget (and it could be as little as £1) it will test your ingenuity and creativity.

One option is to bulk buy items at a supermarket or pound shop – sweets, balloons, novelties – and then simply distribute them in party bags. Alternatively, you could bake your own cakes and biscuits, and use the money to buy one – reasonable quality – wooden toy.

A good joke shop is a source of cheap novelty items for party bags.

Find a source of unusual items that go beyond the usual supermarket clichés. An ethnic shop selling wooden toys from central Europe, embroidered bags from China, beads from India or yo-yos from South America is a good option. Most shops will give you at least a 10% discount if you're bulk buying.

Be creative with the bags themselves. You could buy small plain paper carrier bags and decorate them yourself – maybe with your child's help. Children love it if their bag is decorated with their own names.

Remember that children can be surprised and delighted by very unexpected things, so go for originality, not value.

PARTY GAMES

Organised party games will ensure that your child's party goes with a swing, but they'll need some careful planning. Don't let the games take over; children will also want time to play together informally.

If you have a party theme (e.g. dinosaurs, princesses, super-heroes) adapt the party games to the theme. You could try, for example 'pin the tail on the dinosaur' (rather than donkey) or change 'Duck, Duck, Goose' to 'Princess, Princess, Knight'.

Be adaptable. Some games won't work very well. If you detect signs of boredom and restlessness, move on, don't persist in carrying on with your plan to the bitter end. Be organised, and ensure that you have all the games ready before the children arrive. You're going to be the arbiter, so make sure you understand all the rules.

Don't let things get too competitive. Very young children haven't learnt to be good sports, and may be very sore losers, especially if they see a desirable present disappearing from their grasp.

You could consider giving all the children 'prizes' just for participating, rather than singling out a lucky prize-winner after every game, which may leave some of the children feeling repeatedly left out.

Kitchen Gardens, Flowers & Herbs, Easter Baking, Hot Cross Buns, Egg Hunts

A Day at the Races, Opera Festivals, A Glamorous Opera Picnic, May Buffets

March 21st — June 21st

As the balmy spring breezes and April showers brush away the winter cobwebs it's time to focus on renewal. Now is the time to plant out flowers and vegetables, enjoy delicious seasonal treats such as asparagus and new potatoes, and plan some outdoors fun. From Easter egg hunts and country walks to Flat racing and country house operas, spring is all about rediscovering the pleasures of the open air and socialising again after the more introverted pleasures of late winter. A generous sprinkling of bank holidays will help to get the season off to a flying start.

The Best of Spring

After the sparse winter months, spring sees the first flush of leafy fresh vegetables and some much-anticipated seasonal treats. Over the coming months, produce comes in and out of season, providing plenty of choice and interesting ideas for cooks.

SPRING TREAT: BRITISH ASPARAGUS

May sees the much-anticipated arrival of British asparagus. Choose firm stems with tight, closed buds on the tips. Break off the woody ends, and boil for a few minutes in salted water until slightly softened but still firm – you're aiming for a crunch with each bite. Serve with a twist of black pepper, hot melted butter or Hollandaise sauce.

SPRING TIP: ALPHONSO MANGO

April and May see the fleeting visit of the prized Indian Alphonso mango. With their buttery, soft flesh, and sweet, rich flavour, these mangoes are seen as some of the finest in the world. For the best value, buy by the box from Indian supermarkets and convenience stores.

SPRING HIGHLIGHT: MORELS

These are considered to be some of the finest wild mushrooms. They should be thoroughly washed before use as they can be gritty (they grow in sandy areas), and must be cooked before eating (they are mildly toxic when raw). They make a perfect accompaniment to steak and lend themselves to an excellent sauce. Alternatively, fry some in butter and serve on toast.

Seasonal Produce
Asparagus
Carrots
Cauliflower
Celeriac
Chicory
Clams
Crab
Jersey Royal potatoes
Kale
Leeks
Lemon sole
Mussels
New potatoes
Parsley
Pears

SEASONAL VASE
Hyacinth
Lily-of-the-valley
Muscari
Narcissi
Tulip

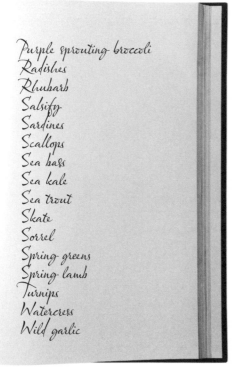

Purple sprouting broccoli
Radishes
Rhubarb
Salsify
Sardines
Scallops
Sea bass
Sea kale
Sea trout
Skate
Sorrel
Spring greens
Spring lamb
Turnips
Watercress
Wild garlic

SEASONAL SPECIALS

The WATERCRESS season begins in April. With its crisp, green stems and spicy, mustardy tang, watercress is highly nutritious and believed to be an aphrodisiac. It makes an excellent salad, garnish, fish accompaniment and soup. It doesn't store very well, so eat as soon as possible.

April also sees the start of the JERSEY ROYAL harvest. Jersey boasts light and well-drained soil, and farmers use seaweed as a natural fertilizer. The result is the distinct flavour and delicate skins of the Jersey Royal new potato. Try them simply boiled or steamed.

PURPLE SPROUTING BROCCOLI is at its best in early spring. Choose firm stems and fresh, green leaves and avoid any that look wilted or yellow. Purple sprouting broccoli is best cooked in salted water or gently steamed; also try it stir-fried with ginger.

SPRING GREENS are the first cabbages of the year, but they remain soft and tender as, unlike cabbages, they do not grow a heart. Cooked correctly they are a delicious, nutritious vegetable. Roughly chop the leaves and thinly slice the stems (they are sweet and tender) and try it steamed or stir-fried.

A Kitchen Garden

Home-grown vegetables taste delicious and will supply a range of fresh, seasonal treats for your table. There are plenty of varieties of vegetables that can be grown quickly and easily, even in a small space. Start off with the easy options – courgettes, runner beans, tomatoes – and try something new each year.

If you are short of time and undercover space, find a good garden nursery and buy plants that are ready to go. It may be more expensive, but it's easier than growing everything from seed. They should be planted in a sunny position, in soil that has been enriched with compost (either general purpose or homemade) or well-rotted manure.

Don't plant out your seedlings until any risk of frost has passed.

Even if there is a heat wave in May, for most of the UK there is a risk of frost until the beginning of June. Broad beans, which are hardy, are the only seedlings that are risk-free. Keep beds free of weeds – remove by pulling up by hand or use a hoe. Don't be tempted to water a little and often; it's best to give your vegetables a thorough soaking to encourage deep root growth. Only water root vegetables – such as parsnips and beetroot – if the soil is extremely dry. Don't forget to label your plants – it's very difficult to identify small plants and it's wise to keep a note of varieties for future reference.

An Easy Vegetable Garden

BEETROOT

Sow direct April–July, about 2 cm deep.

Soak seeds overnight. Sow carefully and not too densely, thinning to approximately 8 cm apart. Beetroot should be harvested once the roots are the size of a golf ball. Sow every few weeks for a successional supply.

BROAD BEANS

Sow in root trainers Feb–April. Plant out April–June, 30 cm apart, in rows 60 cm apart.

Plants may need staking, and blackfly is a common pest. Pinch out the top of the main stem when the first flowers begin to turn into pods. They are ready to pick when you can feel suitably-sized beans inside the pod.

CARROTS

Sow direct April–July, about 2 cm deep.

Once the leaves appear and reach a few centimetres in height, thin to about 5 cm apart. Beware of carrot fly – only thin plants when it's wet weather, or use horticultural fleece to protect them.

COURGETTES

Sow undercover in small pots April–May. Plant out May–June, 60 cm apart.

Courgettes will grow rapidly to a large size, and each plant should produce approximately 20 fruits. Keep picking to encourage more, and don't overlook the edible flowers. Plants are prone to powdery mildew.

CUCUMBERS

Sow undercover March–May. Plant out May–June, 60 cm apart.

Plant out into compost-enriched soil. Plants grow surprisingly large and like to scramble, so are best supported by a bamboo cane. Keep well watered, and pick regularly to encourage new regular fruiting.

FRENCH BEANS

Sow undercover in root trainers April–July. Plant out May–August, 30 cm apart.

There are two types of French bean: dwarf and climbing. Dwarf varieties usually support themselves, whereas climbing varieties will need a bamboo structure to grow up. Pick regularly and you will encourage new growth.

PARSNIPS

Sow direct April–May, about 2 cm deep.

Parsnip seedlings should be thinned to 15 cm between plants, and then left to their own devices. They won't be ready for harvesting until the autumn – it's said that frost will help to sweeten their flavour.

RUNNER BEANS

Sow undercover in root trainers April–June. Plant out May–July, 30 cm apart.

Runner beans should be grown up a tepee of bamboo canes. Plants will produce a substantial crop, and beans should be picked regularly to promote new growth.

SPRING ONIONS

Sow direct March–June, about 3 cm apart; cover with a fine layer of soil.

Spring onions are very easy to grow, and do not need too much thinning out. Sow a new row every few weeks to ensure a constant crop.

SWISS CHARD

Sow direct April–July, about 2 cm deep.

Swiss chard is expensive to buy yet easy to grow. Plants should be thinned to a final distance of 30 cm apart. Pick leaves from the outside of the plant, so new growth will continue in the middle.

TOMATOES

Sow undercover in small pots February–April. Plant out April–June, 60 cm apart.

Tomatoes need lots of sun; try growing a small cherry tomato variety. Stake each plant with a bamboo cane, and pinch out side shoots between the main stem and larger leaves. Feed with tomato food once the first flowers appear.

Planting a Flower Garden

Your garden is an extension of your home, a place that can be used for al fresco entertaining, or simply as a beautiful backdrop. It can also provide you with fresh herbs, and cut flowers and greenery throughout the year. Plan ahead and enjoy some horticultural hospitality.

SETTING THE STAGE

If you're planning to eat outside in the summer, ensure that you have created an area of your garden that is sheltered and secluded, perhaps by utilising a wall, tree or hedge. Think about creating a temporary summer arbour, using annual climbers, such as sweet peas, morning glory or black-eyed Susan, in pots. You will then be able to benefit from full spring and autumn sunshine.

Make sure that guests can sit in dappled shade in the summer.

Plant for visual impact – you can enhance your dining area by planting lavish and colourful displays of annuals in pots or hanging baskets and using them to 'set dress' your patio. Fragrant plants will greatly enhance the dining experience; be wary of plants with a strong, unpleasant odour – avoid Ginkgo trees and flowering currant.

Keep flower arrangements for the dining table low and compact.

GROWING HERBS

Even if you don't have enough room in your garden for herbs, they will thrive in pots on your patio or windowsill. You can buy cheap potted herbs in supermarkets, break up the clotted roots, and plant them out and they will grow surprisingly well.

INDISPENSABLE HERBS
Parsley, sage, oregano, rosemary, thyme, dill, fennel, chives, marjoram, basil, coriander.

BRINGING THE GARDEN INDOORS

Plan ahead and your garden will brighten up your home throughout the year. If you have plentiful supplies of variegated ivy, lady's mantle (*Alchemilla mollis*) and shrubs such as spotted laurel (*Aucuba janponica Crotonifolia*) you will never be short of foliage.

Cut lavender in June and dry upside down in cool places. You can use bunches of dried lavender to decorate and scent your house throughout the year.

PLANTING FOR FRAGRANCE

SPRING:
Lilac,
Wallflowers,
Bearded iris

SUMMER:
Climbing honeysuckle,
Mock orange shrub,
Oriental lily,
Lemon verbena,
Climbing roses (e.g. Buff Beauty, William Morris, Climbing Masquerade),
Night-scented phlox (*Zaluzianskya ovata*),
Sweet peas,
Sweet williams,
Heliotrope (Cherry Pie),
White alyssum,
Stocks (Brompton or East Lothian),
Nicotiana (be sure to get a scented variety e.g. *sylvestris* or *alata*),
Salvia gregii (late summer into autumn)

AUTUMN:
Magnolia grandiflora,
'Glory Flower'
(*Clerodenrum bungei*)

PLANTING FOR DECORATION

SPRING:
Solomon's Seal, Tiarella,
Shrub honeysuckle
(*Lonicera tatarica*),
Spirea bridal wreath,
Euphorbia polychroma,
Dicentra
('love-lies-bleeding'),
Giant Alliums (e.g. *Allium schubertii* or *christophii*)

SUMMER:
Campanula persicifolia,
Camomile daisy, Penstemon,
Foxgloves, Crocosmia (e.g. Lucifer). *Roses always make a traditional English flower arrangement*

AUTUMN:
Lacecap hydrangeas,
Chrysanthemums.
If you cut the flowers of salvia and campanula in the summer they will re-flower in the autumn.

WINTER:
Lonicera fragrantissima (Winter-flowering honeysuckle).
Use dried flower heads from the garden, e.g. Alliums, hydrangeas and Nigella.
Plant bulbs in pots to bring inside, e.g. Iris reticulata.

Before inviting guests, dead-head your plants and remove weeds. Water plants in pots to ensure that your displays are not wilting.

Easter Baking

With a hint of spring finally in the air, Easter is a welcome break after the dreary post-Christmas winter months. The long weekend provides the perfect occasion to spend some relaxing time with family and friends, but no Easter gathering would be complete without hot cross buns and, for those who are a fan of marzipan and dried fruits, simnel cake.

HOT CROSS BUNS

Traditionally spiced with cinnamon, nutmeg, allspice and cloves, hot cross buns should be served hot or toasted, and always eaten on Good Friday. The cross on top of the bun – formed either by cutting the dough or adorning the bun with piped lines of pastry – is said to represent the Crucifixion.

There are many superstitions surrounding hot cross buns. It is believed that hot cross buns baked on Good Friday will never go mouldy; when taken taken out to sea they protect against shipwreck; when hung in a kitchen they ensure perfectly baked bread and protect against fire; when shared with another person they guarantee friendship.

Hot Cross Buns Baking Tips

Try dusting both your hands and work surface with flour, or lightly oiling them, to prevent the mixture from sticking when it's kneaded. Properly kneaded dough should be smooth and springy with an elastic quality.

Hot cross buns!
Hot cross buns!
One ha' penny, two ha' penny,
Hot cross buns!
If you have no daughters,
Give them to your sons
One ha' penny,
Two ha' penny,
Hot cross Buns!

TSOUREKI

This sweet Greek Easter bread is traditionally formed of three thick strings of dough that are plaited together, and garnished with red-dyed hard-boiled eggs. Tsoureki is flavoured with a special Greek spice called *mahleb*, made from the pits of wild cherries.

Always allow enough time for the dough to prove properly (usually 40 minutes to an hour depending on the environmental temperature). Under-proved buns won't bake well, and will come out hard and small.

If you have any left-over hot cross buns going stale, try making an alternative bread and butter pudding. Add a little brandy, orange zest or chocolate to give it an extra flavour.

SIMNEL CAKE

Simnel cake is fruitcake with a twist – a layer of marzipan is included in the middle of the cake, and the cake is also 'iced' with a layer of marzipan, then adorned with little marzipan balls.

Simnel cake was traditionally baked for Mothering Sunday (the middle Sunday of Lent), when girls in domestic service would go home to visit their mothers and take a simnel cake with them. Over the years, this tradition died out and simnel has become associated with Easter.

ELEVEN, TWELVE OR THIRTEEN?

Marzipan balls on top of a simnel cake represent Jesus and the apostles, but the number on top of the cake varies: 13 represents Jesus and the 12 apostles; 12 represents just the disciples; 11 represents the disciples minus Judas.

Simnel cake recipes call for the marzipan balls on top of the cake to be browned under the grill. If you have mastered the art of the kitchen blow torch, use this instead to create a perfectly toasted topping.

"I think of the garden after the rain;
And hope to my heart comes singing,
At morn the cherry-blooms will be white,
And the Easter bells be ringing."

'Easter Bells', Edna Dean Proctor

Easter Entertainments

Easter is a time of year that symbolises fertility and rebirth, but for many of us – especially our children – it's a chance to over-indulge in chocolate. If you're looking for Easter weekend entertainment, it might be a good idea to moderate the chocolate orgy with some old-fashioned traditions, such as egg painting and an Easter egg hunt.

EGG PAINTING

The tradition of painting hard-boiled eggs in the spring pre-dates Christianity, and for many cultures eggs symbolise new life and re-birth. For thousands of years Iranians have painted eggs on Nowruz, the Iranian new year that coincides with the spring equinox.

Chocolate Easter eggs originated in France and Germany in the 19th century.

In Christian tradition the egg is symbolic of the resurrection of Jesus Christ. Eggs took on extra significance at Easter, since it was customary for Christians to abstain from eating eggs and meat during Lent, and Easter was the first opportunity to break their fast.

In England decorated Easter eggs have a long historical pedigree. In Edward I's household accounts for 1307 there is an entry of: "18 pence for 450 eggs to be boiled and dyed or covered with gold leaf and distributed to the Royal Household".

The word EASTER is said to have to come to us from the Norsemen's Eostur, Eastar, Ostara, and Ostar, and the pagan goddess Eostre, all of which are associated with the season of the strengthening sun and new birth.

AN EASTER EGG HUNT

Children will enjoy their Easter eggs all the more if they have to hunt for them. All you'll need is plenty of small, wrapped Easter eggs and a basket or bowl for each child so that they can stow their booty.

If your children are small, it's probably best to just hide the eggs and allow them to roam free and hunt. Tell the children that they must return to base when they have a certain number of eggs (e.g. six); this will allow you to check that the eggs are being fairly distributed between all the children.

Older children will love responding to written clues. You can use brightly coloured craft cards, which you tape to strategic trees or walls — kids will enjoy rhyming couplets or terrible puns. Alternatively you can give each child a written sheet of clues that will direct him/her to key points around the garden.

Agree beforehand that the children can eat a small number of eggs at the end of the hunt, but must take the rest home with them to eat later.

HOW TO PAINT AN EASTER EGG

- You will need: eggs, food colouring, vinegar, rubber bands, an empty egg carton, white wax crayon.

- Hard boil your eggs in a saucepan of water for 10 minutes. Remove from the heat and add cold water to cool the eggs.

- Half-fill a cup with water, a teaspoon of vinegar and a teaspoon of food colouring.

- Use a crayon to draw designs on your egg. If you then dip the egg in the cup of dye, the wax will remain white, highlighting the design against the coloured background.

- You can make a stripy egg by placing rubber bands around the egg before dipping.

- Once you've lifted your eggs from the dye, place them in the egg carton to dry.

EGG HUNT ETIQUETTE

- Pair up older and younger children to ensure that everyone has a chance.

- Keep an eye open for children who are struggling with clues and help them.

- Keep a few eggs back to redress imbalances.

- Chocolate rationing is essential if you want to avoid hyper-active kids.

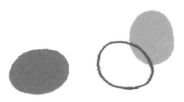

A Walk in the Country

A beautiful spring day is ideal for a country walk but remember to abide by the unwritten rules of behaviour, observed in the British countryside for many centuries, to ensure that you don't enrage landowners, or upset the locals in the pub. There's an age-old way of doing things in rural Britain…

COUNTRYSIDE RULES

Plan ahead, especially if you're taking an unfamiliar route. Look at a map (never rely on using your mobile phone as reception may be patchy) and check that you are suitably equipped for the weather. Set off in good time and, in the winter months, think about how long the walk will take and consider what time you will lose daylight. Never attempt any portion of a countryside walk in the dark.

Make sure you are well-prepared before you undertake a long walk.

Stand aside to let people pass if the path is very narrow or if you are going slower than them, and always give way to fellow walkers who are coming uphill. Stick to designated paths, especially in crop fields, and leave gates as you find them – they will be open or closed for a reason. Wild or farmland animals shouldn't be approached, and dogs should be kept on a lead when you are in close proximity to animals.

Always walk on the side of the road facing oncoming traffic.

When rounding a bend or blind corner, move to the other side of the road to avoid head-on collisions, and then move back to face the oncoming traffic on a straight stretch. When driving in the country, be patient. Keep to your side of the road, and don't let reduced visibility tempt you into wandering into the oncoming lane. If you are stuck behind slow-moving tractors or agricultural machinery, resist the temptation to flash your headlights or swing out from behind. Drive very slowly when horses are on the road.

Greet people you encounter with a friendly smile or "Hello".

RESPECT THE ENVIRONMENT

It goes without saying that you should never drop litter or leave dog mess. Don't start a fire, drop cigarette butts or use a disposable barbecue. Think about your actions and the impact they may have upon nature and wildlife.

Pub Etiquette

GET YOUR ROUND IN

A roaring fire, stack of Sunday newspapers, a few sleepy dogs and the hushed tones of village gossip at the bar are fundamental to the quintessential English country pub. As a visitor, however, remember to observe the subtleties of pub etiquette.

First of all: observe drink-buying rules. If a group of you are drinking together it is usual for people to take it in turns to buy a round. Don't opt out of rounds, or hang back; you shouldn't have to be asked.

GO WITH THE FLOW

Respect the unique atmosphere of the pub. If your fellow drinkers are sitting alone or in couples quietly chatting and reading papers, don't ruin the mood with loud banter or uproarious games of darts and bar billiards. Pubs are very sociable places so be prepared to exchange small talk with strangers.

On the other hand, if a solitary drinker is lost in contemplation of their pint or crossword, respect their privacy – if they want a chat they'll make it obvious.

RESPECT THE LOCALS

Don't hog a space at the bar, blocking the way for other punters. Observe the unwritten 'first come, first served' rule and never try to attract the bar staffs' attention by waving money or clicking your fingers.

Be aware of 'regulars'. These are habitual customers of the pub, who might have their own favoured seat, special glass, or repartee with the barmaid. The pub is their second home, so respect their prior claims.

PAYMENT PRIORITIES

Tipping is not necessary in a pub if you've only had a drink. However, if you feel you've received particularly notable service you may like to offer the bar staff a drink. If you've eaten and enjoyed table service, you should leave a tip for the waiting staff (about ten per cent).

If you're hosting guests for the weekend you should pay for the pub lunch (unless another arrangement has been agreed). If you're splitting the bill, divide it equally; niggling about the comparative cost of dishes and drinks looks cheap.

"There is nothing which has been yet contrived by man, by which so much happiness is produced as by a good tavern or inn."
Samuel Johnson

All about Racing

Before you consider hosting or attending a day at the races, equip yourself with some basic knowledge, and you'll be able to carry off a well-informed conversation with aplomb.

Horseracing in Britain dates back to the reign of James I in the 17th century when members of the court helped to establish Newmarket as the home of organised racing. James I purchased what is now the Rutland Arms in Newmarket High Street and built the first royal palace in the town. The royal association with Newmarket continued into the reign of Charles II – the Rowley Mile was named after his favourite hack, 'Old Rowley'.

Three of the Classics races, which pitted 3-year-old horses at the peak of their fitness over shorter distances, the St Leger, the Oaks and the Derby, were all founded between 1776 and 1780. But it was not until the 19th century that horseracing became popular with the general public, following the advent of steam trains, which made racetracks widely accessible. Today annual attendance at British horseracing events exceeds 6 million, and at least £10 billion is bet on racing each year.

DATES FOR YOUR DIARY

The National Hunt, or 'Jump racing' season runs from autumn to spring. It comprises Hurdles and Steeplechasing.

The Flat racing season runs from May to September. The five Classic races are the Newmarket 2,000 and 1,000 Guineas Stakes, the Epsom Oaks and Derby and the Doncaster St Leger. Royal Ascot is the pinnacle of the Flat racing season.

Happy Birthday! All thoroughbreds have their birthdays on 1 January.

~ Horseracing: A Bluffer's Guide ~

Also-ran A horse that finishes 'down the field' in a race (i.e. out of the prize money).

Blown up When a horse starts to drop out of contention in a race due to lack of fitness.

Broken down When a horse sustains an injury – normally a tendon/soft tissue injury requiring a long rest to recover.

Bumping Interference during a race where one horse collides with another.

Checked When a horse's run during a race is momentarily blocked by another horse or horses.

Clerk of the Course The person responsible for the overall management of a racecourse.

Clerk of the Scales The person who checks a jockey's weight against the permitted weight the horse can carry.

Length The length of a horse from its nose to the start of its tail. Also used to describe the winning margin.

Nose Smallest official distance a horse can win by.

Off the pace When a horse isn't keeping up in a race.

On the bridle Describes a horse running comfortably, still having a bite on the bit.

Paddock/Parade Ring The area where horses can be viewed prior to a race.

Pecked/Nodded When a horse's head nearly lands on the ground after jumping a fence.

Penalty Additional weight carried by a horse on account of previous wins.

Ping 'To ping' is to jump in particularly good style.

"He's pinging those fences!"

Colours Shirts or 'silks' worn by jockeys to identify a horse with a particular owner.

Conditions The make-up of a race, as in the number of runners, the ground conditions, if it's a sharp or a galloping track, etc.

Cut in the ground Also called 'soft going' when there is 'give' in the ground surface.

Distance The length of a race: 5 furlongs (5 x 220 yards) is the shortest, 4½ miles is the longest.

Draw A flat racing term denoting a horse's position in the starting stalls.

Favourite The horse in a race with the shortest (smallest) odds. Also called the 'market leader' and 'the jolly'.

Field, the Term for the runners in a race.

Going, the The conditions underfoot on the racecourse.

Handicap A race in which each horse carries an allotted weight to equalise all the runners' chances.

Handy A horse who is in a prominent racing position.

Pulled up A horse that does not finish a race.

Pulling When a horse fights the jockey by pulling against the bridle.

Run free A horse going too fast too early, which then can't settle into the race.

Scope A horse that is likely to improve with age and as it grows into its frame.

Spread a plate When a racing plate or horseshoe comes off, and the horse has to be re-shod.

Stayers Horses with a lot of stamina who are more likely to show up best over 3 miles.

Steeplechase A race over fences, ditches and water jumps.

Stewards The group of people responsible for ensuring adherence to the rules of racing.

Valet A person responsible for looking after a jockey's equipment.

Weigh in/out Weighing the jockey before and after the race to make sure the horse carried the right weight.

A Day at the Races

You'll enjoy your trip to the horseraces all
the more if you're appropriately dressed,
well-informed and know what to expect and
how to behave. And remember, a hearty
picnic will set up both you and your guests
for the long afternoon ahead.

STYLISH DRESSING

Adhere to the correct dress code for the enclosure for
which you have a ticket. Racegoers will be turned away if
they're inappropriately dressed.

A day at the races is a special occasion and you should dress
smartly. Men should wear a suit, or jacket, in both cases
with a tie. Ladies should choose a smart dress or suit (steer
clear of miniskirts, halter necks and spaghetti straps). It's
fine to wear trouser suits (or a matching top and trousers).
Remember there will be a lot of standing around, so
toe-pinching stilettos might not be the best choice. Spring
and summer race meetings can be quite chilly so bring a
smart pashmina or jacket to avoid goose pimples.

Always double-check the correct dress code.

An ideal choice for gentlemen race-goers is the Panama hat
– particularly stylish with a linen suit. Wear it low over the
brow, with a slight tilt, and if you're intent on showing
your good manners, hold it by the crown and raise it a few
inches from your head when greeting a lady. Some race
meetings are an occasion when ladies can wear all kinds of
extravagant hats and fascinators. If you've chosen to wear a
wide-brimmed hat, avoid a brim-crushing collision by
steering clear of kissing similarly-dressed counterparts.

THE KNOWLEDGE

Backing one or two horses to place will, in the long run,
not offer you the same returns as betting on three or four
horses to win. Avoid outsiders, but if the going is heavy,
form generally means nothing – an outsider can be worth a
punt. Study the form guides and look for a horse that has
improved gradually. Listen to betting shop and trackside
chatter and keep an eye on any horse that is being well
backed. Set yourself a betting limit and stick to it.

If you can't afford to lose the money, don't bet.

Talk Tic-Tac
Tic-tac: the sign language
used by bookmakers to
communicate changes in betting
odds on the racecourse.

Score: £20
Pony: £25
Ton: £100
Monkey: £500

Burlington Bertie: 100-30.
Carpet: 3-1.
Cockle: 10-1.
Double carpet: 33-1.

Remember elaborate hats might block other people's view of the action.

Knock: to owe money and not pay up
Rock cake: a small bet
Beeswax: tax
Bismarck: a favourite that bookmakers expect to lose.
Drifter: a horse whose odds get bigger just before the race due to a lack of support in the market.
Backed in: a horse on which lots of bets have been placed, resulting in a decrease in the odds offered.
Shortening odds: bookmaker's reduction of the odds on a particular horse.

If you've staked your money on a loser, don't sulk or give way to petulance. Accept your loss with equanimity and move on. If you're a lucky winner, enjoy a quiet sense of satisfaction, but don't gloat or get over-excited. Less fortunate punters will find your antics wearisome.

Of course, you will find the race exciting (especially if you've backed a real contender) but keep loud shouting or excited screaming to the minimum, especially if you're very close to other people. After the race, there'll be a large number of people gathering around to collect their winnings – wait patiently in line or come back later.

RACEDAY HOST
Picnics are often taken at the car before the first race. If you're in charge it's best to keep it simple – salmon, ham, pâté and fresh bread, a classic Quiche Lorraine, potato salad (try adding capers, chopped mint and minced anchovies) with a bowl of salad (bring your vinaigrette in a screwtop jar). A coolbox of champagne, wine, beer and soft drinks will get your racing party going with a swing.

This hearty fare should set your guests up for a long afternoon of racing thrills and the inevitable visits to the bar. Make sure you pace yourself and moderate alcohol intake with water, soft drinks and snacks.

Keep your guests well supplied with form guides and ensure they can sit down, relax and enjoy the refreshments on offer – an afternoon at the races can be very tiring.

> "Horse sense is the thing a horse has which keeps it from betting on people."
> W. C. Fields

A Night at the Opera

You may not be an opera aficionado but there's no need to feel excluded from this most elevated of art forms. Armed with some basic knowledge of terminology and with the help of programme notes, plot summaries and even surtitles, you should be able to hold your head up in the world's finest opera houses.

A GUIDE TO OPERA ETIQUETTE

Arrive on time Most opera houses won't let you in after the opera has begun. You may have to wait in the foyer until the intermission, so don't be late.

Shush! Don't ruin the drama by whispering, coughing, rustling sweet-papers or humming along.

Mobiles off Allowing your mobile to ring out during an opera performance will be regarded as a capital offence by opera-lovers. Play it safe and switch it off before you go into the auditorium.

Bravo! It's quite normal to clap after a particularly well-executed aria. You could even shout "Bravo!" (or "Brava" for a female). If in doubt, observe your fellow audience members and follow suit.

Applause essentials Clap when the conductor takes to the podium (at the very beginning and after the interval), after the overture, at the end of an act, and at the final bows. Avoid whooping, whistling or braying – feet stamping is a definite no-no.

Dress appropriately Unless it's a major gala performance or a country house opera there are no dress codes, though many patrons will enjoy dressing up for a special occasion. Jeans, trainers, shorts and flip-flops will be frowned upon.

> { "No good opera plot can be sensible, for people do not sing when they are feeling sensible." }
>
> W.H. Auden

Ten Essential Operas

CARMEN, *Bizet* (Paris 1875)
A sultry love triangle set in Seville

DON GIOVANNI, *Mozart* (Prague 1787)
A murderous lothario keeps a date with death

EUGENE ONEGIN, *Tchaikovsky* (Moscow 1879)
Romantic wires are crossed in the Russian countryside

JULIUS CAESAR, *Handel* (London 1724)
A tale of derring-do set on the banks of the Nile

LA BOHÈME, *Puccini* (Turin 1896)
A tear-jerker set amongst artists in Latin Quarter Paris

LA TRAVIATA, *Verdi* (Venice 1853)
A frail tart with a heart teaches lessons in moral values

RIGOLETTO, *Verdi* (Venice 1851)
A hunchbacked court jester gets his come-uppance when his daughter is seduced

THE BARBER OF SEVILLE, *Rossini* (Rome 1816)
An old man is hoodwinked by a clever barber so that a loving couple are united

THE FLYING DUTCHMAN, *Wagner* (Dresden 1843)
A salty ghost story set at sea

THE MARRIAGE OF FIGARO, *Mozart* (Vienna 1786)
A philandering count is forgiven by his long-suffering wife

~ Opera: A Bluffer's Guide ~

Aria A long, emotional solo sung by the main character of an opera.

Baritone A male singing voice, higher than a bass but lower than a tenor.

Bass A male singing voice, the lowest in the scale.

Bel Canto A style of Italian singing or an opera written in such style that emphasises phrasing, tone, and technique.

Buffo The comedian of an opera; comes from the Italian term for 'buffoon'.

Cabaletta A faster, more upbeat, second half of an aria.

Cadenza A segment at the end of an aria that shows off a singer's vocal ability.

Canzone A folk song used in a opera, usually sung by the *buffo* in a comedic way.

Libretto Refers to the words in an opera.

Maestro Refers to the conductor, whether male or female.

Melodrama A passage of work that involves alternating dialogue with song.

Mezzo-Soprano A female singing voice, lower than a soprano but higher than an alto.

Opera Buffo A performance that focuses on ordinary people; sometimes it is comedic in nature.

Opera Seria A performance that focuses on gods, goddesses, and heroes; considered a 'serious' opera.

Parlando Singing that sounds like ordinary speech that may occur in the middle of an aria.

Patter Song A song in which an actor sings an excessive number of words in a short amount of time.

"An excellent Cavatina but a disappointing Cabaletta."

Cavatina The slower, first half of an aria.

Coloratura Fast notes and trills up and down the scale; a style that began in the baroque era.

Contralto A female singing voice in the lower vocal range.

Countertenor A male who elevates his voice to alto pitch.

Double Aria An aria with two parts, the slower cavatina, and the faster cabaletta.

Embellishment The act of adding notes to a melody line.

Grand Opera Refers to an opera without any spoken dialogue; utilizes a large orchestra and chorus.

Interlude A short piece of music, instrumental, played between acts or scenes in an opera.

Leitmotiv A recurring musical sound that precipitates the appearance of a particular character or event.

Prima Donna The leading lady in a theatrical production.

Recitative A song that is sung in a conversational style.

Répertoire A block of performance of pieces that a company can perform without any further preparation.

Roulade A quick run of notes sung on a single syllable.

Soprano A female singing voice of the highest vocal range.

Supertitles Used during foreign operas, they are the texts projected on a screen above the stage (also called surtitles).

Tenor A male singing voice of the highest vocal range.

Tremolo Refers to a rapid reiteration of pitch.

Trouser Role A role of a young man or boy that is sung by a female.

Vibrato Refers to a wavering of frequency of pitch while singing a single note.

Country House Opera

With spectacular surroundings and world-class performances, country house opera is a highlight of the British Season. Performances begin in the late afternoon or early evening to allow time for an extended interval during which the well-dressed audience enjoy a stylish picnic supper.

The host should be responsible for organising all the details of the picnic.

If it is a sizable party, the host can divide the catering responsibilities between the guests, but he/she must be specific to avoid mismatches or duplications. It is sensible to take picnic chairs, as it's especially difficult to sit on a rug elegantly when wearing an evening dress, and a table is a welcome addition. Opt for a linen tablecloth and napkins, and proper wine glasses, champagne flutes and cutlery (never plastic). A cool box is a must on warm evenings; maintain a traditional feel with a willow picnic basket with leather accents for crockery and china.

Nothing beats a pre-performance glass of bubbles in the gardens.

Arrange a meeting place for the whole party and take a stroll around the grounds. Allow extra time to secure a good picnic spot in the gardens; if it is windy, make sure everything is well battened down. If the weather looks changeable, grab an undercover spot in good time (you can sometimes book in advance) as dry space will be at a premium. Take a warm shawl to fend off the chill of the evening. Late spring nights can be quite cold.

Simplicity is best: serve easy-to-eat treats, finger-foods and ready-cut portions.

The picnic is eaten during the interval, usually 90 minutes. Classic British spring and summer delicacies (asparagus, smoked salmon, strawberries) that can be elegantly nibbled with minimal mess usually fit the bill. Pack in ordered layers, with pudding that the bottom and pre-performance nibbles at the top. Include a bag for rubbish, and a tea towel for unexpected spills. White wine, rosé and champagne must be served chilled (don't forget a corkscrew), and offer plenty of non-alcoholic options.

Think about the practicalities of carrying picnic equipment from the car park.

May Bank Holiday Buffet

May is a generous month, providing two bank holidays and, hopefully, a glimmer of summer. With the decent weather and milder temperatures, it's the perfect time to think about entertaining for larger numbers. As soon as the dining table gets too crowded, think about the option of a buffet. With advance preparation, buffets are the most relaxed and convivial way to eat, both for hosts and guests.

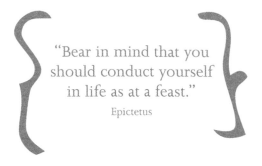

"Bear in mind that you should conduct yourself in life as at a feast."
Epictetus

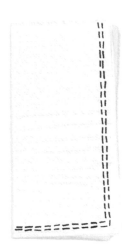

When planning a buffet, there are a number of practical considerations. You need space for a large table, and room for guests to freely move along to serve themselves. Placing the table in the middle of the room provides access from both sides. You also need room for people to be able to eat comfortably, rather than being packed in like sardines. It's essential that they can sit down to eat. Allocate a separate, well-stocked bar area to avoid congestion.

Never rely solely on the weather – a back-up plan of a mini marquee or awning is a must – and if it's freakishly hot, food won't react well to being exposed to the heat of the sun for hours. As a general rule, two hours is enough for any dish at room temperature.

Make it straightforward for guests to serve themselves. Place the mains and side dishes so it is simple to see what's on offer, and is easy to serve oneself without stretching over other guests. Pre-roll cutlery in napkins to be collected at the end of the table so that guests don't have to hold too many things while they are helping themselves to food. Plates should be in a prominent position, and always put too many out – no one wants to feel like they are last.

When guests have finished, make sure that you have a tidying-up plan in place. There is nothing worse that a room littered with dirty plates, or guests clutching on to their plates because there is nowhere to put them down. Clear up promptly before pudding comes out, and do a second sweep once pudding is done.

BUFFET GUEST ETIQUETTE

- Don't be the first one, vulture-like, loading-up your plate when the food is served.

- Offer to serve other people if you're holding the serving spoon and standing next to each other.

- At a buffet, the pace at which you eat is less crucial than at a table, but make sure you don't end up being the last one chewing.

- Plates shouldn't be overloaded – it's better to go back for seconds than to look like you haven't eaten for a week. Equally, there's a limit to how many times you should be returning for more…

Buffet Checklist

- Make sure there is plenty of seating; assume that most people will want to sit down to eat.

- Plan simple and popular dishes that mix and match well, but don't go overboard. Two to three main courses, along with an interesting selection of side dishes, is plenty.

- Lay the table logically. Guests will need start at one end with plates and main dishes, proceed to side dishes and salads and finish with cutlery.

- Choose dishes that can withstand being prodded and poked at with a serving spoon – impressive structures look good untouched, but turn into unappetising messes.

- If guests are socialising outside in the sun, make sure there is plenty of shade.

- Always over-cater and remember that often guests will eat more at a buffet than a sit-down meal.

- Everything should be fork friendly – choose food that doesn't require any cutting with a knife.

- Check guests' dietary requirements and make sure there is a balance of meat, fish and vegetables.

- Make sure dishes are full to capacity. Food looks more appetising when there's lots of it.

- Provide plenty of bread so that guests with extra-large appetites can easily fill up.

- Little touches count – garnish the dishes, put out plenty of sauces, dressings and pickles.

- Keep an eye on dishes and replenish or remove as soon as they are running low.

Buffet ideas

Roast Scottish beef
Coronation chicken
Glazed Gammon
Lemon and honey chicken
Poached salmon
Quiche Lorraine
Courgette and goat's cheese tart
Exotic leaf salad
Potato and chive salad
Coleslaw
Fine bean salad
Greek salad
Waldorf salad
Cous cous salad
Tomato and Mozzarella
Pesto pasta salad

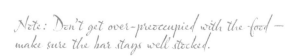

Note: Don't get over-preoccupied with the food – make sure the bar stays well stocked.

S U

Summer Lunch, Cricket Club Tea, Homemade Pimm's, A Day at the Beach

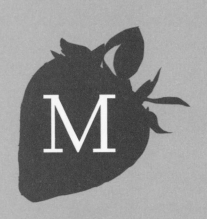

M M

A Summer Barbecue, Garden Games, Music Festivals, The Glorious Twelfth

E R

June 21st — September 21st

The long, lazy days of summer are the season for lingering games of croquet and cricket, trips to the beach, or more leisurely stays in holiday cottages and villas. Adapt your entertaining to summer's sensual pleasures. Enjoy your garden and eat a simple al fresco meal with friends, as the twilight descends and the night-scented stocks perfume the air. Indulge in fresh barbecued fish or home-made kebabs, seasonal salads and a glut of summer fruits, from tart gooseberries to luscious raspberries. And don't forget classic summer drinks such as sangria and Pimm's.

The Best of Summer

Summer brings some of the seasonal highlights of the year. The long days and warm temperatures come together to provide a glut of fresh fruit and vegetables. This is the time to make the most of seasonal eating at its best.

SUMMER TREAT: THE PERFECT SIDE SALAD

Create a colourful and interesting salad by using seasonal baby leaves such as red chard, mizuna, young spinach, rocket, sorrel and red mustard. Keep the dressing fresh and simple by drizzling over a little balsamic vinegar, some good extra virgin olive oil and a squeeze of lemon. Serve as soon as possible to avoid wilting.

SUMMER TIP: PICK YOUR OWN

Find a local farm that offers 'pick your own' fruit; strawberries and raspberries are the most usual. Strawberries can be picked from June until August in a good summer, and raspberries are most plentiful during July. Also look out for farms that offer redcurrants, blackcurrants and gooseberries.

SUMMER HIGHLIGHT: SAMPHIRE

Samphire is available from fishmongers over the summer months. Marsh samphire is the tastiest and most readily available (rock samphire is harder to come by) and is a succulent, salty treat to accompany fish dishes. If picked very young, it can be enjoyed raw; alternatively boil and serve tossed in melted butter with a squeeze of lemon.

Seasonal Produce
Aubergines
Blackcurrants
Broad beans
Broccoli
Cabbage
Carrots
Cauliflower
Chard
Cherries
Courgettes
Cucumber
Dover sole
Fennel
Gooseberries
Green beans

SEASONAL VASE

Agapanthus
Cornflower
Delphinium
Peony, Rose
Sweet Pea

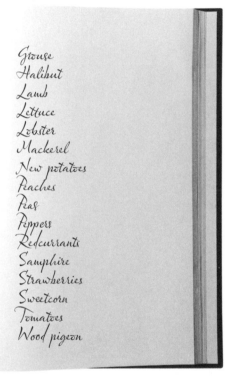

Grouse
Halibut
Lamb
Lettuce
Lobster
Mackerel
New potatoes
Peaches
Peas
Peppers
Redcurrants
Samphire
Strawberries
Sweetcorn
Tomatoes
Wood pigeon

SEASONAL SPECIALS

The short British CHERRY season runs for about four weeks from late June. With cherry orchards in decline in the UK, British cherries are harder to come by so hunt them out at your local farmers' market or watch out for pop-up stands on the sides of rural roads.

The MACKEREL season is at its peak during July; it is an inexpensive and easy to come by fish. Signs of freshness include bright eyes, firm flesh and shiny skins. Try grilling a whole fish on the barbecue — it is delicious served with horseradish or a gooseberry sauce.

Don't overlook COURGETTES as the summer months bring an abundance of these tasty cucurbits. Try to buy them as small as possible and, if you are lucky, with the flower still attached. Avoid boiling them and, instead, try them sautéed or griddled.

Fresh BROAD BEANS are available over the summer months, and offer an intensity of flavour that is hard to beat. Freshness is key; look for firm, crisp pods. Fresh broad beans are best served boiled (they cook quickly) — if you have the time, pod the beans from their skins too.

An Al Fresco Summer Lunch Party

If the weather's warm, an outdoor lunch is a real summer highlight. But don't stick to your guns if the clouds roll in or the wind picks up. Shivering around a table as rain spatters your summer salad is an absurd display of Blitz spirit.

Create a light, seasonal menu that won't involve hours sweating in a hot kitchen.

Eating outside on a summer's day is a good opportunity to lay on some seasonal salads, perhaps accompanied by a classic Quiche Lorraine or savoury tart. Exploit fresh vegetables such as courgettes, beetroot, fennel, peas, green beans, new potatoes, tomatoes and watercress.

If we're enjoying a rare heat wave, why not follow the Mediterranean practice of providing a mezze – a mixed platter of bread, cheese, olives, cold meat and salad. Make tomato bruschettas by brushing sliced ciabatta with oil, then griddling or grilling the bread until charred and golden. Rub the bread with a clove of garlic and then spoon over a mixture of chopped tomatoes, olive oil, salt and black pepper. Top with a sprig of basil.

This delicious bread can be accompanied by a platter of Parma ham, salami and olives. You could also grill slices of halloumi, then drizzle them with olive oil, which you have infused with lemon juice and oregano, before serving.

Try a Summer Pudding, a delicious confection of bread soaked in juicy berries.

Summer brings a great range of delicious fruits – most people will be delighted with a generous bowl of strawberries or raspberries and cream. Alternatively, you could provide a classic gooseberry fool. Top and tail 450g/1lb of sharp gooseberries and put them in a pan with 3 or 4 tablespoons of sugar and 2 tablespoons of water. Bring to the boil, simmer for 10 minutes then leave the fruit to cool, and mash it up with a fork. Hand-whisk about 300ml/half a pint of double cream until it feels thick and heavy. Then fold in the cooled fruit.

Squeeze fresh lemons and add sparkling mineral water and sugar to taste.

Provide soft drinks or water as well as alcohol, so that guests can pace themselves over the long afternoon.

A Classic Quiche Lorraine

Serves 6

1. Sift the flour and a generous pinch of salt onto a cold surface. Cut the butter into 1cm cubes and stir it in, then gently squeeze the two together, so the flour combines with the lumps of butter – so it turns into crumbs.

2. Sprinkle a little of the water over the top and stir it into the mixture. Add enough water to bring it into a dough (unless your kitchen is very dry, you probably won't need it all), then cover with clingfilm and refrigerate for 20 minutes.

3. Lightly flour a work surface and shape the dough into a rectangle. Roll it out until 3 times its original length.

4. Fold the top third back into the centre, then bring the bottom third up to meet it, so your dough has three layers. Give the dough a quarter turn and roll out again until 3 times the length, fold again as before, and chill it for 20 minutes.

5. Preheat the oven to 180°C/gas mark 4 and put a baking tray in to warm. Grease a deep (at least 3cm) 20cm tin, and line it with the pastry. Line with foil and weight down with baking beans. Place on the baking tray and blind bake in the oven for 40 minutes, then remove the foil and beans. Bake for a further 8 minutes, then brush the base with egg white and put back into the oven for 5 minutes.

6. Fry the bacon for 8–10 minutes, until cooked through, but not crisp. Drain and spread half over the hot base.

7. Put the cream and the eggs and yolks into a large bowl with a generous pinch of salt, and beat together slowly until combined, then give it a fast whisk for 30 seconds until frothy. Pour over the base to fill and then sprinkle over the rest of the bacon. Bake for 20 minutes – it's done when it's puffed up, but still wobbly at the centre. Allow to cool slightly before serving – hot quiche tastes disappointingly bland.

For the pastry base:
225g/8oz plain flour
225g/8oz cold butter
100ml/3.5fl oz iced water

For the filling:
200g/7oz dry cure smoked streaky bacon, chopped
320ml/11fl oz double cream
4 eggs and 2 egg yolks (use 1 egg white for brushing the pastry)

Note: Use any ingredients you have lying about in your quiche: cheese, leek, spinach, flaked salmon...

Essential Cricket

If you don't know your bouncer from your full toss or your googly from your gully, you may need to swot up on this most arcane of English sports. Whether you're attending a test match or watching your local team play on the village green, the sound of leather against willow will inevitably evoke the quintessential English summer.

> "It's a funny kind of month, October. For the really keen cricket fan, it's when you realise that your wife left you in May."
> Dennis Norden

THE INS AND OUTS OF CRICKET

Cricket is played between two teams of 11 players on a grassy field, in the centre of which are two wickets. When a team is 'in' they are batting, and the other team, which is bowling and fielding, attempts to get each of the batsmen 'out'. Each 'over' consists of six consecutive balls, bowled from one end. Finally the team that was 'in' is 'all out', and takes its place in the 'outfield'. The team that was in the out field goes 'in' until they too are 'all out'. This process (an innings) may be repeated once more (a match can last one day or take as many as five). The team with the highest number of 'runs' (points scored primarily by running between wickets after hitting the ball) wins the match.

ESSENTIAL ETIQUETTE FOR CRICKETERS

- The Umpire's decision is final. Never show any dissent.

- Walk when given out — no lingering or arguing.

- Applaud the new batsman as he makes his way to the wicket.

- Never interfere with the seam or surface of the ball (polishing is fine).

- Never deliberately distract the batsman.

- No dangerous bowling: never risk causing physical injury to the batsman.

- No time-wasting.

~ Cricket: A Bluffer's Guide ~

All out The batting team is said to be all out when ten of its eleven batsmen are dismissed. The eleventh batsman cannot continue without a partner.

Appeal The fielding side's invitation to the umpire to give a batsman out.

Bails The two pegs that are held horizontally in grooves at the top of the stumps. The bails and stumps together comprise a wicket.

Batting order The order in which the members of a team go out to bat.

Beamer A fast, head-high full toss.

Bouncer A fast, shortpitched ball, bowled to rise off the pitch to the height of the batsman's chest or head.

Inswinger Swing delivery that moves in the air towards a right-handed batsman.

Leg-break A ball spun by the bowler so as to turn from leg to off for a right-handed batsman.

Leg-bye Run scored from a ball that hit the batsman's body rather this his bat.

Leg cutter Fast bowler's delivery that leaves the righthanded batsman sharply after pitching.

Leg side The side of the pitch nearer the batsman's legs as he faces the bowler, i.e. to the bowler's right for a right-handed batsman.

Leg spinner A bowler whose primary delivery is the leg-break.

"He's just bowled a maiden over."

Bowled An 'out' that is achieved by a ball that hits the wickets, whether or not it is touched by the bat.

Cover Run-saving fielding position, in front of the wicket on the off side. Hence extra cover (straighter), cover point (squarer).

Drive A straight-batted, front-foot batting shot, in front of the wicket.

Duck When a batsman is out without scoring any runs.

Full toss A ball that reaches the batsman without bouncing.

Googly A wrist-spinner's off-break, bowled with an action similar to that for the leg-break.

Gully Fielder in catching position, slightly behind square on the off side.

How's that? The Marylebone Cricket Club law book's prescribed form of words for an appeal to the umpire to give a batsman out (often shortened to "Howzat?").

Maiden An over in which no run is scored off the bat, nor from a wide or no-ball.

Night watchman A lower order batsman sent in to 'stall for time' in the late evening.

Off-break A ball spun by the bowler so as to turn from off to leg for a right-handed batsman.

Off-cutter Fast bowler's delivery that turns sharply towards a right-handed batsman after pitching.

Seam bowler Bowling technique that causes the ball to deviate by landing the seam on the pitch.

Silly Prefix added to name of fielding position to indicate that it is very close to the bat, e.g. silly mid-on, silly point.

Sticky wicket A field which is partly dry and partly wet, creating a treacherous and uncertain bounce.

Yorker A ball that is bowled and lands at or near the feet of the batsman instead of bouncing at a normal distance.

A Cricket Club Tea

The life of village cricket teams revolves around the cricket club tea – a chance for members of the team to take a break and socialise with wives, children and other onlookers. If you've volunteered to join the tea rota then homemade cakes will endear you to everyone – a selection of scones, fruit cakes, chocolate cakes and lemon cakes will suit every palate.

You should cater for, at the very least, 22 players, 2 umpires and 2 scorers. But remember, some cricket club teas are popular with wives and children, and numbers can be unpredictable. Always err on the generous side. Ensure that the sandwiches are plentiful and the tea is hot and your efforts will be appreciated by players and spectators alike.

Most cricket clubs will have a hot water urn and will keep supplies of tea bags, sugar and squash.

Shopping List
4 loaves medium sliced bread (2 brown, 2 white)
Butter (2 × 400g/14oz)
Cheese, (to be served with pickle or cucumber)
12 eggs (for egg mayonnaise)
Ham or corned beef
2 tins of tuna or salmon
Mayonnaise
Pickle
Cherry tomatoes
1 cucumber
Milk (3 pints/1.5 litre)

You will need to make the tea at the start of the last over (ask one of the waiting batsmen to tip you the nod). This will ensure it is fresh and piping hot.

Crisps
Sausage rolls
(buy 10 large rolls and cut them into small pieces)
Cakes or homemade scones:
(allow for 2 scones or 2 slices of cake per person)
Chocolate biscuits

Remember to bring washing–up liquid and tea towels as you'll have to clear up when the players are back on the pitch.

HISTORICAL CRICKETING MILESTONES

When the talk turns to cricket impress fellow club-members with your knowledge of the salient dates in cricketing history.

1550 (approx) Evidence of cricket being played in Guildford, Surrey.

1598 Cricket mentioned in Florio's Italian-English dictionary.

1624 Jasper Vinall becomes first man known to be killed playing cricket: he was hit by a bat while trying to catch the ball at Horsted Green, East Sussex.

1676 First reference to cricket being played abroad, by British residents in Aleppo, Syria.

1697 First reference to 'a great match' with 11 players a side, in Sussex.

1709 First recorded inter-county match: Kent v Surrey.

1710 First reference to cricket at Cambridge University.

1744 First known version of the Laws of Cricket, issued by the London Club, formalising the pitch as 22 yards long.

1780 The first six-seamed cricket ball, manufactured by Dukes of Penshurst, Kent.

1787 First match at Thomas Lord's first ground, Dorset Square, Marylebone.

1806 First Gentlemen v Players match at Lord's.

1814 Thomas Lord's third ground opens on its present site, in St John's Wood.

1836 (approx) Batting pads invented.

1845 First match played at The Oval.

1859 First touring team to leave England draws enthusiastic crowds in the USA and Canada.

1873 W.G. Grace becomes the first player to record 1,000 runs and 100 wickets in a season.

1877 First Test match: Australia beat England by 45 runs in Melbourne.

1880 First Test in England: a five-wicket win against Australia at The Oval.

1882 Following England's first defeat by Australia in England, an 'obituary notice' to English cricket in the *Sporting Times* leads to the tradition of The Ashes.

Summer Classics

The warm summer months introduce a change in our eating habits. Hot days and balmy nights mean that we choose to eat lightly, picking at seasonal treats and putting together light dishes. This is the time to take it easy, and enjoy the weather and long evenings, rather than slaving over the stove.

Choose easy family meals and entertain simply – make the most of interesting sharing plates, quick dips and indulgent fruity puddings. Fresh, local produce will be in abundance, so get down to your local farmers' market and make the most of seasonal summery vegetables, salads and fruits.

Glasses can be kept fresh and interesting with some classic summer drinks – Pimm's, sangria and ginger shandy. Be prepared for some impromptu summer drinking, so make sure there is always a crisp bottle of white wine in the fridge, as well as ice-cold lagers and, for those special occasions, a bottle of good bubbly.

SIMPLE SANGRIA
Perfect proportions…
3 parts red wine
1 part orange juice
2 parts lemonade

Mix it up…
Taste and adjust the proportions accordingly. Place some ice in a large jug and add the sangria.

Classic garnish…
Garnish each glass with some fresh mint and a few slices of orange or lemon.

GINGER SHANDY
Perfect proportions…
1 part ginger beer
1 part lager

Mix it up…
Place some ice in a glass, squeeze over some fresh lime juice, add the ginger beer and lager.

Classic garnish…
A quarter of a lime.

Summer is the perfect time to enjoy a drink or two al fresco.

Homemade Pimm's
Perfect proportions…
2 parts red vermouth
2 parts gin
1 part Cointreau

Mix it up…
Combine 1 part of the mixture with 2 parts lemonade in a large jug and stir.

Classic garnish…
A few mint sprigs, some thinly sliced cucumber, lemon and orange, a few quartered strawberries.

Light Bites for Summer

HUMMUS
200g/7oz canned chickpeas
2 garlic cloves, crushed
2 tbsp lemon juice
1 tsp ground cumin
100ml/3.5fl oz tahini
4 tbsp water
Salt
Olive oil
Paprika

Place the chickpeas, garlic, lemon juice, cumin, tahini and water in a food processor. Blend until smooth. Season to taste, adding more lemon and cumin if required. Serve, drizzled with olive oil and sprinkled with the paprika, with fresh, warm pitta bread.

GAZPACHO
1kg/2lb 3oz tomatoes, diced
1 cucumber, peeled and diced
2 cloves garlic, crushed
150ml/5fl oz good olive oil
100g/3.5oz stale white bread
2 tbsp sherry vinegar
Mint leaves, finely chopped

Blend the tomatoes, cucumber, garlic and olive oil in a food processor. Soak the bread in cold water for 20 minutes, squeeze out any excess moisture then add to the mixture in chunks. Blend and chill thoroughly. Add the vinegar and season to taste. Garnish with mint leaves, some diced cucumber and a swirl of olive oil.

BABAGANOUSH
1 aubergine
3 tbsp olive oil
2 garlic cloves
Juice of half a lemon

Pierce the skin of the aubergine, and place under a hot grill or over the flame of a gas hob. Grill until the skin is blackened and allow to cool. Scrape the flesh from the charred skin and combine with the rest of the ingredients in a food processor and blend to form a rough paste. Serve with warm flatbread or ciabatta.

BEETROOT AND FETA SALAD
3 raw beetroots
2 shallots
1 tbsp fresh lemon juice
1 tbsp olive oil
75g/2.6oz feta
Mint leaves

Heat the oven to 180°C/gas mark 4. Wrap each beetroot in foil and roast until tender (approximately 1–1.5 hours). Allow to cool, then peel and chop into bite-sized chunks. Finely chop the shallots, and combine with the lemon juice and olive oil. Season to taste. Pour over the chopped beetroot, and crumble over the feta, slightly mixing it all together. Add a final sprinkle of olive oil and garnish with finely chopped mint leaves.

CRUSHED BROAD BEANS
500g/1lb 2oz podded broad beans
Juice and zest of half a lemon
4 tbsp olive oil
Parmesan
Mint

Cook the broad beans in salted water, drain and cool in ice-cold water. Remove the beans from the skins, and then mash with a fork. Add the lemon juice, zest, olive oil. Season to taste, and serve with freshly toasted ciabatta.

COURGETTE FRIES
Courgettes
Flour
Water
Frying oil

Place a few spoonfuls of flour into a mixing bowl and slowly add water, mixing thoroughly, until you have a thick but viscous batter. Cut the courgettes lengthways into little sticks, similar to French fries. Put a few inches of oil into a saucepan, and heat carefully. Drag the courgette sticks through the batter, drop into the hot oil and allow to cook for a minute or two, until golden brown, then drain on kitchen paper. You will need to cook the courgettes in quick batches; season with salt and freshly ground black pepper and serve immediately.

A Day at the Beach

*Four of the Best
Beach Games*

*Twister beach towel
Beach cricket
Frisbee
Bat and ball*

If you're lucky enough to live near the sea, or if you've got a coastal holiday cottage, you may want to invite some friends to join you. Plan ahead and you'll get the most out of a sociable day at the beach.

Pack some vital beach supplies: sunblock, spare hats, towels, hand wipes (useful when the sand is glued to your fingers). Bring folding deckchairs or sun loungers if you've got them; if not, come with plenty of raffia beach mats, inflatable sunbeds and old towels.

Cater for children in the party by bringing plenty of beach toys.

Plastic plates and cups will withstand the sea air better than paper. Most of the food you'll be serving can be eaten with your fingers, but bring real cutlery if possible. Make sure you've got plentiful supplies of napkins or paper towels and rubbish bags.

Respect other people's space and ensure that noise is kept to a minimum.

Copious amounts of ice-cold drinks are an absolute must, so bring a cool box with plenty of bottled water, fruit juice and fizzy drinks for the kids. If you want it to turn into a real party, you can pack wine and beer. Alternatively you can blend spirits (e.g. rum or vodka) with concentrated fruit juices (e.g. orange, cranberry) and freeze overnight.

Pay attention to the coastguard and take note of any signs or flags.

If you've found a really remote location, you'll be able to bring a portable barbecue and turn the air black with charcoal smoke. You'll have to prepare skewers and marinade meat at home the night before and pack it in a cool box. It's best to assemble salads on the spot and add dressing, otherwise they'll be sad and wilted. If you're really lucky you'll be able to buy fresh sardines and mackerel and grill them – the ultimate beach food.

If your dogs are permitted, be extra vigilant and clear up after them.

If you're on a more populated beach, barbecues will be frowned upon. So go for a simple and hearty picnic – e.g. cold roast chicken, Scotch eggs, pork pies and salad. Or you could simply make lots of delicious sandwiches – crabmeat, crayfish or prawns will give a nautical flavour. Sandwiches are easy to eat when it's breezy and sand is drifting about.

Barbecues

The aromatic smells of charcoal-grilled food drifting over twilit gardens are one of the most evocative signs of summer. A barbecue is a fantastic opportunity to share the pleasures of a summer evening with friends. But beware, comfortable informality requires forethought, and you should plan carefully to ensure that your guests are able to relax, eat well and enjoy each other's company.

Ensure that the barbecue is lit and ready before guests arrive Panic-stricken recourse to paraffin can be discouraging, especially when guests are hungry, so plan ahead. Make sure that everything is prepared before the start of the event: you should arrange the seating, serving table, cutlery and crockery well in advance.

Provide plentiful supplies of ice-cold water.

Keep all the food you're going to barbecue in the fridge until it's time to start cooking – in hot weather food will soon deteriorate, and you don't want to poison your guests. Ensure that you have plenty of ice, and that drinks are well refrigerated. Water will keep your guests hydrated, and may prolong the supply of chilled beer and wine. Remember, hot sun and spicy food will make your guests thirsty.

Inform your neighbours of the upcoming event or invite them.

Barbecues are highly aromatic and, depending on wind direction and cooking ability, neighbours may find themselves suffocated by acrid black smoke or tantalising smells. Try and site your barbecue as far away from the house as possible, or at least ensure that the barbecue is upwind of near neighbours.

{ "My first outdoor cooking memories are full of erratic British summers, Dad swearing at a barbecue that he couldn't put together, and eventually eating charred sausages, feeling brilliant." }

Jamie Oliver

Barbecue: "To broil or roast (an animal) whole;
e.g. to split a hog to the backbone, fill the belly with wine and stuffing,
and cook it on a huge gridiron, basting with wine". OED, 1861

Comedy aprons, chef's hats and swaggering machismo as
the meat hits the grill are obtrusive and self-centred. Your
guests have come to eat and socialise, and should not feel
coerced into applauding a one-man show.

Find out beforehand if any of your guests are vegetarian.

Barbecues are about the pleasures of al fresco eating, not
discomfort. Juggling food and drink while standing will
diminish your guests' enjoyment. So make sure that all
your guests have a drink in hand and a place at a table, with
adequate cutlery and napkins, before you start barbecuing.

Don't leave your guests waiting around for food.

If you're catering for vegetarians make sure you have plenty
of salads, and dips such as hummus or tzatziki. Ensure that
you have prepared thoroughly beforehand — preparing dips,
sauces and salads, marinading meat and fish, threading
kebabs on skewers and so on — so that you can keep a
steady flow of food from grill to plate.

Don't force your guests to tough it out in a cold, windswept garden.

Accept offers of help from your guests — either with
cooking, serving drinks or handing food round. A barbecue
is an informal gathering, so encourage guests to help
themselves to bread, salads and drinks.

Always make contingency plans to move indoors if
necessary. If the weather is disappointing, use the kitchen
grill to cook your barbecue food. It's not ideal, but it would
be foolish to ignore the vagaries of an English summer.

Garden Games

Combine a summer lunch party with some traditional garden games and you'll find your guests will still be there as the shadows lengthen, enjoying both your hospitality and their own competitiveness. Just make sure you lay on plenty of cold drinks, and intersperse the games with regular breaks, so that guests can refuel, sit down and relax.

CROQUET

Dating back to the 14th century, croquet originated in France, where it was called *paille-maille*, meaning 'ball-mallet'. The French passed their enthusiasm for the game on to their Scottish allies, and James I of England (James VI of Scotland) introduced the game to the London court. Pall Mall in London owes its name to nightly games of croquet played there by King Charles II and his court.

Paille-maille was adapted by a French doctor who renamed it 'croquet' after the crooked stick used to hit balls through hooped wickets. In 1868 the formal rules of croquet were codified and it became popular all over the British Empire.

The basic aim of the game is for competing teams to hit balls through a circuit of 12 hoops and finish by hitting the peg. The blue and black balls are played against the red and yellow balls. Each player's turn consists of a single stroke, unless the player successfully hits the ball through the hoop or makes a 'roquet' (i.e. hits another ball), in which case the player gets another two strokes. With the first of these strokes the striker is allowed to hit the roqueted ball.

Attacking the opponent's ball is often the best way to win the game. You will soon find that your guests are gripped by a fierce sense of competition, and the game will be accompanied by rage and hilarity. Lay on plentiful supplies of Pimm's and the afternoon will pass very enjoyably.

Queen Sirikit of Thailand was such a fan
that pétanque became an official sport
of the Thai army.

PÉTANQUE

Inject some Gallic flare into your garden party with this
game that originated in the south of France. In fact, there
was such a craze for boules in that region that King Charles
IV banned commoners from playing it. The present-day
version of boules, pétanque, emerged in Provence in the
early 19th century; the name derives from the Provençal
phrase *a pes tanca*, meaning 'anchored feet'.

Each player starts the game by tracing a circle that is large
enough to stand in. The aim of the game is for each player
to throw a boule at the 'jack', or 'cochonnet', (a smaller,
target ball), without moving outside the defined circle. The
player who gets his boule nearest to the jack is the winner.

As with croquet, there is great scope in pétanque for skill
and skulduggery because players are positively encouraged
to interfere with each other's balls.

You don't have to be a Gitanes-smoking, pastis-swilling
Frenchman to excel at pétanque, and it is eminently
practical since it can be played on any reasonably level patch
of hard ground; a manicured lawn isn't necessary.

Badminton is the fastest racquet sport; shuttlecocks can reach over 200 mph.

LET THE SHUTTLECOCKS FLY

You could always try the more energetic game of
badminton. All you need for the garden version is a net,
racquets and a shuttlecock, and some way of designating
the boundaries of the court. You can play singles or doubles.
Players win a point whenever they win a rally and each
game is played up to 15 points. Rallies are won when the
shuttlecock is hit out of the court or lands on the floor of
the opponent's court. The shuttlecock may only be hit once
before it passes over the net during a single stroke.

It's a fast and furious game that will have your guests
sweating profusely and begging for mercy. Make sure
you have plenty of cold drinks on tap.

Entertaining Outdoors

Jugs of tap water, served with ice and a twist of lemon, will avoid dehydration.

Al fresco entertaining can be one of the highlights of the summer, but you must be hyper-aware of the weather. Only consider eating outside if you're convinced it's warm enough for everyone; you may be a hardy outdoor type, but spare a thought for more sensitive souls.

If you're entertaining at lunchtime, remember not everyone will want to bake in full sunlight, so locate your table in dappled shade under a tree, or make sure you have parasols and spare sun hats. Eating outside doesn't inevitably mean that you have to be uncomfortable. Examine your garden furniture, and if chairs and tables are rickety or stained, think about bringing some of your indoor furniture outside (be sure to bring it in at the end of the evening). Ensure that guests have cushions, so they're not sitting on hard wooden seats. A tablecloth will disguise a multitude of stains and gives the table a festive air.

Have cosy rugs, woollen wraps and spare jumpers ready in case it is chilly.

Think carefully about the logistics of serving the food and drink, and try to minimise the number of journeys you have to make back and forth to the kitchen. If you've got a spare table, set it up outside – it will be useful for serving dishes, wine, jugs of water and so on. Make sure that you have plenty of ice for your ice buckets – there's nothing worse than lukewarm white wine – and use wine cooler sleeves to keep bottles cold. Cold boxes are very useful for storing beer and soft drinks. Ensure that you have a plentiful supply of drinking water.

Lay the table with proper glassware, crockery and cutlery – no plastic plates.

If you're entertaining at night, think carefully about lighting. You can use fairy lights or LED light strips to illuminate your house, or a picturesque tree. But you'll also need to ensure that people have adequate lighting at the table, so that they can see the food and each other's faces. You can go for a variety of mood-enhancing options: tea lights in pretty holders, paper lanterns, Moroccan lanterns or candles, but remember these are not ideal for breezy nights. Self-charging solar garden lights will provide a more stable alternative. Always ensure that the path to the loo is illuminated – you don't want guests stumbling in the dark.

AL FRESCO MENU TIPS

🍷 Don't choose elaborate meals that will involve you dashing back and forth from the kitchen all through the meal. You'll miss out on the fun!

🍷 Try and create a menu that can be prepared in advance and will need minimal attention once your guests arrive.

🍷 Utilise the best of summer food: grilled bream or bass, flash-fried marinaded salmon, prawns marinaded in sweet chilli and ginger, grilled lamb steaks with tsatziki. Follow up with a mouth-watering summer fruit trifle or a classic summer pudding.

🍷 Encourage guests to eat as soon as they're served – food cools down quickly outdoors …

🍷 Remember, if you're eating outside you'll crave stronger flavours, so make strong marinades and sauces using garlic, ginger, chilli, soy sauce and mirin.

🍷 Don't stand on ceremony; dining outside is always going to feel more relaxed, and guests will enjoy serving themselves and fetching and carrying.

{ "There is no spot of ground, however arid, bare or ugly, that cannot be tamed into such a state as may give an impression of beauty and delight." }

Gertrude Jekyll

Music Festivals

It all began with Glastonbury back in the '70s, and today music festivals are an integral part of the summer season. Each festival has its own unique flavour and feel, but either way punters are faced with a few days and nights in a field. The best festival-goers are those who can maintain a carefree, sunny spirit, no matter how deep the mud, but with the changeable British summer weather, preparation and forethought is key…

As the host, you must make sure that everyone in the party has their own ticket, knows which car park to head for and an idea of which campsite to pitch in. Plan contributions for food, drink and equipment, giving each party-member a detailed list. Take a trolley or a wheelbarrow with you too – otherwise you will be making loads of trips from the car to the campsite, which can often be a long way and a waste of precious relaxation time.

Take some time to choose your pitch.

Avoid areas of the campsite that are at the bottom of a hill, near a tap, downwind from the loos or on a main route to the festival arena. Create a social area by the tents where everyone to congregate and relax. Take a plastic-backed picnic rug, gazebo and foldable chairs, and you should be able to sit out, even if the weather is temperamental.

Hang something on your tent so that you can recognise it amongst the hundreds of other tents, and observe some landmarks to help you easily find your way home in the dark (take a torch with you in the evenings). Have mobiles at the ready – it's easy to lose friends amongst the festival crowds, especially in the dark.

Embrace the unique unity that music festivals create.

Introduce yourself to your neighbours and invite them to socialise with you and your party. Be friendly to strangers and be willing to share your things – food, drink, sun cream, umbrellas and blankets.

Festival Equipment
Tent, tent pegs, mallet
Penknife
Mattress, foam sleeping-mat
Ear plugs
Sleeping-bag
Extra blanket, pillow
Eyemask
Towel
Suncream
Deodorant
Toothbrush, toothpaste
Medical kit
Insect repellent
Antibacterial hand gel
Loo paper

Campfires, fireworks and barbecues are normally forbidden. Leave your patch of the campsite just as litter-free and nature-friendly as you discovered it. Find a bin for everything, or hold onto it until you do, and try to recycle wherever possible.

Waterproofs
Wellies
Flipflops
Plenty of clothes
Plenty of socks, warm jumpers
Sunglasses
Hat
Bottle opener
Lighter
Torch
Spare batteries
Plastic bags, string
Gaffer tape
Plastic-backed rug
Foldable picnic chairs
Gazebo

"It always rains on tents. Rainstorms will travel thousands of miles, against prevailing winds for the opportunity to rain on a tent."
Dave Barry

FESTIVAL FOOD

🍷 Remember to eat and to stay hydrated. Keep an eye on everyone in your party and make sure they are kept well-fed and watered.

🍷 You will inevitably eat fast food during the weekend, but a few snacks and drinks that you've taken along with you will be a welcome change.

🍷 Take along some sultanas, flapjacks, fruitcake and cereal bars. Don't take anything that can go off or that needs to be kept cool.

🍷 Some festival-goers take a camping stove so they can boil up some water for tea and warm up some beans for supper. Remember you'll need to bring cutlery, plates, mugs, saucepans and so on.

🍷 Take plenty of water. It's a good idea to equip yourself with a really big bottle for teeth-cleaning, washing etc., and then some smaller bottles for drinking.

🍷 Glass is usually prohibited, but cans are allowed in the camping areas. Make sure you recycle.

🍷 Take cash for drinks and food, as stalls often don't take cards. Keep your valuables safe, and don't leave money in your tent.

Holiday Cottage Entertaining

Don't take advantage of your friends, turning them into housekeepers and babysitters

The fantasy of enjoying a week or two in a fabulous holiday cottage or villa with a few close friends is extremely seductive. But remember, the undoubted bonuses of sharing your holiday space with a crowd of people can all too often be offset by petty disputes and ill-feeling.

DIVIDING THE SPOILS

If you are the prime mover, i.e. if you found the property, administered the rental and organised the holiday guests, then you have earnt special status. You are entitled to choose your own bedroom, and other guests should recognise this and give you priority.

Don't let yourself get caught up in a land grab; allocate rooms beforehand.

If the rental is a cooperative venture, you might find that you're racing your fellow guests, trying to get to the property first and secure the best accommodation. This undignified battle can ruffle feathers at the outset and cause a poisonous atmosphere. It's better if you can sit down with your fellow guests beforehand, look at the property brochure or website, and try and allocate rooms on the basis of need. For example, a couple with a baby might need a larger bedroom; an elderly relative might prefer a room on the ground floor and so on.

COOPERATIVE LIVING

Discuss catering arrangments at the outset. It's pointless to set up a rigid cooking rota and then find that one of the guests is a passionate cook, who loves nothing better than sourcing and preparing local produce, and resents every minute he or she is shut out of the kitchen. In a situation like this, it would obviously be wise to make way for the enthusiastic cook.

Tailor the catering arrangements to your guests' preferences and abilities.

Clearly, if nobody is stridently demanding kitchen privileges, then it is sensible to take it in turns to prepare the main meal, and it is obviously easiest if the person who is cooking is also responsible for shopping. If you're adamantly anti-cooking, or resent being expected to prepare meals on your holidays, then you should treat your fellow guests to a meal out.

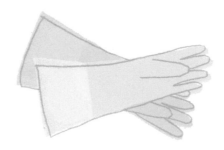

SHARED RESPONSIBILITIES

You can be sure that nobody will want to take total responsibility for washing up, tidying and cleaning, so this is an area where it is essential that everybody shares the chores, and this should be made clear at the very beginning. If one person is washing up day after day, while fellow guests loll unthinkingly on their loungers, then resentment is an inevitability, and holiday good spirits will evaporate. Watch out for guests who are turning into drudges and stop the rot.

NO BUCK PASSING

Don't look on a shared holiday rental as a chance to palm your children off on your unsuspecting friends. Your children remain your responsibility and, if you need help with them, this has to be negotiated on an ad hoc basis.

RESPECT THE RENTAL

☕ Leave everything as you've found it, dispose of your rubbish and maintain basic cleaning standards while you're in residence.

☕ Think about your neighbours: you might only be in residence for a week or two but your landlord will resent having to pick up the pieces when you've annoyed people nearby.

☕ Be aware of noise nuisance. Treat the place as your own and don't pollute a quiet country neighbourhood with loud music, screaming kids and roaring engines.

☕ If you've brought your dogs, make sure they don't stray into private property, and control loud barking.

☕ Drive carefully; you may be tucked away down a narrow country lane, so don't enrage the locals with crazy driving antics.

The Glorious Twelfth

The opening of the red grouse shooting season on 12 August is famously called the 'Glorious Twelfth'. In the days and weeks that follow, these lean and tasty birds are in demand as restaurants and cooks make the most of this seasonal treat.

Grouse prices are at a premium in the days just after the Glorious Twelfth.

Ensure you are buying wild, rather than farmed, grouse by sourcing the birds from farm shops, butchers and game dealers. It is usual to buy the birds 'oven-ready', but check them for age and quality. Young birds should be fresh-smelling, firm-breasted and sharp-clawed, with a pliable beak, legs and feet. They should also be plump and moist, with unblemished skin. Young birds are best roasted; older birds can be tough and are usually braised or used in rich casseroles, flavoured with thyme and red wine.

You should allow a bird per person; keep it simple and traditional.

Remove the wishbone and, for a tidy-looking result, snip the wings and legs at the second joint. Wipe out the inside of the cavity, stuff with some sprigs of thyme, and season inside and out. Tie the legs with string and, as an optional extra to protect the breast meat, place a couple of rashers of bacon around the bird. Preheat the oven to 200°C/gas mark 6. Cooking times vary according to the age of the bird (and the strength of your oven); young ones take approximately 20 minutes, older birds can take up to 40 minutes.

To ensure accurate cooking times, cook grouse from room temperature.

Grouse should be served rare; the breast meat should be springy but not too soft. Always allow the meat to rest for at least ten minutes before serving. Grouse is traditionally served with gravy (made from the cooking juices), bread sauce, redcurrant sauce, game chips or game crumbs. Purists often cook the grouse liver inside the cavity of the bird and spread it, like pâté, on a little crouton and serve it with the roast. Grouse is best suited to red wine; try a Burgundy (such as Gevrey-Chambertin) or a northern Rhone (such as Côte Rôtie).

A generous garnish of watercress is a classic accompaniment.

THE GAME SHOOTING SEASON
Grouse: 12 August–10 December
Partridge: 1 September–1 February
Pheasant: 1 October–1 February

GAME LAWS
In England, Wales and Ireland, no game may be killed on Sundays and Christmas Day. There are no restrictions in Scotland, but it is not customary to shoot game on these days. Game may not be shot at night (between one hour after sunset and one hour before sunrise).

GROUSE SHOOTING
Only found in the British Isles, red grouse grow up in a natural moorland habitat and are not reared by gamekeepers. They are one of the most difficult birds to shoot and are therefore one of the most alluring to the sportsman – British grouse shooting is famous all over the world. The majority of shoots take place on the moors of northern England and Scotland; there is a strict code of etiquette and behaviour on a grouse shoot.

CHIPS AND CRUMBS
Game chips and game crumbs are a traditional accompaniment to classic roast grouse. To make game chips, cut a large potato (Maris Piper works well) into very thin slices (preferably using a mandolin). Gently heat some oil and, when hot, fry the potato slices for three to four minutes, until crisp and golden. Drain on a piece of kitchen roll and season with salt. For game crumbs, fry two handfuls of white breadcrumbs in six tablespoons of butter until they are crisp and golden.

A

U

Back to School, Halloween Traditions, Stocking the Larder, Bonfire Night

T

U

Squash Soup, A Tea Drinker's Guide, Perfect Scones, A Sunday Roast

M

N

September 21st — December 21st

As the leaves fall and the weather turns stormy, it's time to retreat indoors and enjoy autumnal pleasures. Fruits and nuts can be picked, preserved and pickled, ready for the long winter ahead. As the nights draw in, you can enjoy the cosy pleasures of drawn curtains, a roaring fire and a steaming hot casserole, fragrant with herbs and packed with fresh root vegetables. Now is the season for prolonged Sunday lunches and indulgent afternoon teas. And the evenings of autumn are set alight by bonfires, fireworks and Halloween horrors.

The Best of Autumn

As the long days of summer start to fade, autumn arrives with a surprisingly tantalising array of treats. Often blessed with a few days of warm sun and bright skies, the autumn months have plenty to offer, so indulge in the season's specialities before winter sets in.

AUTUMN TREAT: KENTISH COBNUTS
Keep an eye out for cobnuts – a cultivated variety of hazelnut – mostly found in Kent and known as the Kentish cobnut. Unlike most nuts, cobnuts are eaten fresh (wet). Try them roasted, buttered or salted. Alternatively they are a great addition to an autumnal salad.

AUTUMN TIP: PERFECT ROAST PHEASANT
With a similar texture to chicken and a milder flavour than other game birds, a roasted pheasant will always be a popular choice. Roast the bird, wrapped in bacon, breast-side down, paying special attention to the cooking times, and allow to rest before serving. One bird should feed two to three people.

AUTUMN HIGHLIGHT: BLACKBERRIES
Head out to the hedgerows and go blackberry-picking. Ripe fruits should be black, glossy and slightly swollen; pick carefully to avoid 'bursting' the berries. Eat on the same day as picking, or freeze immediately. Traditionally, it is seen as bad luck to pick blackberries after Michaelmas Day (29 September).

Seasonal Produce
Apples
Beetroot
Blackberries
Cabbages
Cobnuts
Curly kale
Damsons
Duck
Figs
French beans
Grouse
Guinea fowl
Jerusalem artichoke
John Dory
Leeks

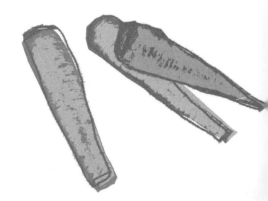

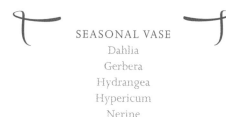

SEASONAL VASE
Dahlia
Gerbera
Hydrangea
Hypericum
Nerine

SEASONAL SPECIALS

Surprisingly sweet and aromatic, PARSNIPS are a versatile and tasty root vegetable. Medium-sized are the best, as larger ones can be fibrous. Roasted parsnips are a classic accompaniment to a traditional roast, but also try parsnip mash, chips and crisps.

Look out for some unusual varieties of APPLES and PEARS which are at their best during late autumn. The best varieties of late pears include Concorde, Doyenné du Comice and Conference. Look out for Egremont Russet, Crispin and Laxton's Superb apples.

FRESH FIGS are available from late summer into autumn. The fruits are extremely delicate, so avoid ones that feel very soft, are bruised or have a strong smell. Aside from enjoying as a sweet fruit, they make the perfect accompaniment to Parma ham and goats' cheese.

With a distinctive appearance and flavour, JERUSALEM ARTICHOKES are inexpensive and versatile. They can be roasted, sautéed, baked, boiled or steamed, used raw in salads, and also lend themselves to a deliciously satisfying autumnal soup.

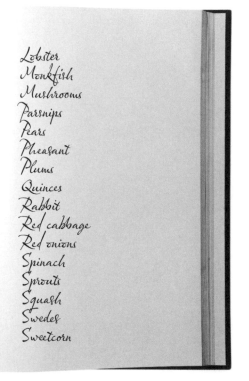

Lobster
Monkfish
Mushrooms
Parsnips
Pears
Pheasant
Plums
Quinces
Rabbit
Red cabbage
Red onions
Spinach
Sprouts
Squash
Swedes
Sweetcorn

Back to School

The summer holidays have run their course and it's time to send your children off to school. You will find yourself caught up in the relentless ritual of nourishing breakfasts, packed lunches and the inevitable invitations to friends to come round for after-school tea.

If a child visitor refuses to try your food, accept with good grace. Don't ply the child with extra snacks or fizzy drinks.

AFTER-SCHOOL TEAS

It's vital to invite your children's friends round to your home. It's part of a social contract, which will ensure that your own children receive invitations, and a major step in the social education of your children.

If you're inviting another child around after school, the first issue you'll have to consider is food fads. Even if you've managed to persuade your own child to keep an open mind in relation to food and a willingness to try anything once, this will not inevitably be the case with schoolfriends.

If you are informed that the child has a ridiculously restricted diet, or one that you regard as unhealthy, bite your tongue. This is not the place for missionary zeal and the best you can do is provide the preferred foods (or a version of them), even if you don't really approve of them. Take food allergies seriously.

Remember, no child is going to starve if he/she refuses the food you're offering. Don't run yourself ragged trying to find alternatives that are acceptable – it's good for children to learn that being a guest involves being accommodating.

Don't let your standards slip completely – it will confuse your own kids. If you find guests helping themselves to food from your fridge or changing your TV channels, just as if they were in their own home, be firm and insist that they ask you first.

Children's favourites
Fishfingers or fishcakes
Sausages
Spaghetti Bolognese
Macaroni cheese
Chilli con carne (easy on the chilli!)
Shepherd's pie
Roast chicken
Homemade burgers
Pizza
Corn on the cob
Baked potatoes
Chips

Don't suspend your own house rules just because you've got guests.

Never embarrass your child in front of his/her fellow pupils or teacher. Behaviour that is acceptable in the privacy of your own home may be absolutely mortifying in a school context.

Finger food: carrot and cucumber 'matchsticks', cherry tomatoes, cheddar cheese cubes, salami, fresh bread and butter.

Don't overload the kids with fizzy drinks, crisps, biscuits and cakes.

Ask children's mothers what they will and will not eat.

HOW TO BE A RESPECTABLE PARENT

- Turn up for regular meetings with the teacher. Pleading that you're 'too busy' to discuss your child's progress will be a real black mark against you.

- Always fill out all the material that comes from the school, and promptly (double-check your child's bag every day for communications from the school).

- Always turn up for end of term concerts, school plays, carol services etc. Your child will care desperately if you don't attend.

- Give a little time to the school – it may be manning a stall at the school fête, putting together a newsletter in the evenings, or helping out on a school trip.

- Try your best to answer all appeals for help from the school – be it for cash contributions, food for the harvest festival, old clothes for school plays, gifts for a sister school in Africa.

- Never storm into the school at the end of the day and berate your child's teacher. If you have a concern, always make an appointment.

Halloween Traditions

Poised between the autumn and winter, Halloween is a time of celebration and superstition. As the nights drawn in and the leaves wither and fall it is an atmospheric time to indulge in the spine-chilling pleasures of ghost stories and enjoy some thoroughly spooky festivities.

The origins of Halloween are often associated with the ancient Celtic festival of Samhain, although there is little evidence that the Gaelic festivals held in the autumn were ceremonies for the dead. It is more probable, therefore, that perceptions of Halloween as a time when the veil between the living and the dead is lifted and ghosts wander the earth are linked with the Christian festivals of All Saints and All Souls. In fact, Hallows is an archaic English word for saint – hence All Hallows Eve, the last night of October.

In the Middle Ages it was a commonly held belief that those who died unabsolved of their sins would be condemned to wait in Purgatory, and that living friends and relatives could release them from this state by praying, collecting alms and attending mass. On All Souls Day torchlit processions were held, bonfires were lit and churchbells were rung to comfort lost souls.

> "Tis now the very witching time of night, When churchyards yawn and hell itself breathes out Contagion to this world."
>
> *Hamlet*, William Shakespeare

By the 14th century the custom of 'souling' had developed in England. Poor supplicants would go from house to house on All Hallows Eve asking for soul cakes. Small cakes or loaves were donated in exchange for prayers for dead relatives (the origins of trick or treating).

During the Protestant Reformation these customs and observances were driven underground. Soon the festival had taken on more occult and demonic associations, which were disapproved of by the Church of England.

The widespread adoption of Halloween customs in the USA did not really take place until the 20th century, and at first trick or treating was disapproved of as ritualised begging. It did not become a widely accepted until after the 1950s. Since then, aided by Hollywood and US television, Halloween has become an increasingly popular ritual in many countries worldwide.

Tip: Don't discard the seeds from your Halloween pumpkin. Roast them in a hot oven (190° C) for 45 minutes, and they'll make a delicious snack.

JACK-O'-LANTERN

The legend of the jack-o'-lantern originated in Ireland. Stingy Jack, who double crossed the devil and was condemned, on his death, to become an eternal wanderer, was given a burning coal by the devil for light. Stingy Jack carried the coal in a carved out turnip and has since been wandering the world.

In Ireland and Scotland, people began to make their own versions of Jack's lanterns by carving scary faces into turnips or potatoes and placing them into windows or near doors to frighten away Stingy Jack and other wandering evil spirits. In England, large beets were used. Immigrants from these countries brought this tradition with them when they went to the United States. They soon found that pumpkins, a fruit native to America, made perfect jack-o'-lanterns.

TOP ETIQUETTE TIPS FOR HALLOWEEN TRICK OR TREATERS

! "Trick or treat?" should be used as an ice-breaking formula, not a real threat. Halloween fun should never feel menacing.

! Children should not be too greedy – if they are offered treats, make sure that they don't take too many and remember to say thank you.

! Stay safe. Make absolutely sure that children don't stray beyond agreed boundaries and wander into streets where they are knocking on strangers' doors.

! Remember, some households may not be as welcoming as others. If there's no answer, don't repeatedly ring the doorbell – move on.

! If you don't mind giving out treats, but would prefer not to have visitors, leave some sweets or chocolate on your front doorstep and let trick or treaters help themselves.

! If you don't want any Halloween visitors, turn out the lights or go out for the evening.

A Children's Halloween Party

Skeletons, bats, witches, blood, ghosts…
Children love everything about Halloween,
from the costumes and decorations to the
spooky food and gory games. Indulge your
kids with a Halloween party to remember.

Keep an eye open for very small children — they might feel genuinely scared.

Your children will enjoy making spooky treats for
Halloween. You can start by making some special cookies.
Make a basic biscuit dough using eggs, plain flour, butter
and caster sugar. Use special Halloween cutters to create
a range of ghoulish shapes. Once the cookies are baked
you can go mad with red and black food colouring and
fondant icing, daubing them with blood, 'ghost writing'
and spider's webs.

Let children help with party preparations. It's all part of the excitement.

Freak out your guests by filling surgical (latex gloves) with
water and freezing them. You can decorate your 'hands'
with blood (red food dye), then float them in a bowl of
fruit punch (cranberry juice is a good colour) or stick them
in a bowl of red jelly.

Let imaginations run riot. Don't be too restrained about décor or costumes.

Children will love mozzarella 'eyeballs'. Just take some
cherry tomatoes, halve them and remove the seeds with
a sharp knife. Cut some mozzarella balls in half, squeeze
them into each cherry tomato half, trimming the edges
to fit. Use black olives pressed into the middle of the
mozzarella to make the pupil.

Extravagantly admire all Halloween costumes, however eccentric.

Decorate your rooms with spider's webs, dangling bats
and spiders, glow-in-the-dark fingers and eyeballs. Use
guttering candles to create an atmospheric ambience and
apply the finishing touches with floating 'ghosts' – balloons
draped in crepe paper, suspended from the ceiling on
invisible threads.

Organised games will help to contain the children's
excitement. Apple bobbing is traditional and easy. Or you
could make a slimy lucky dip using olive-oil covered pasta
shapes, olives and lychees (and some wrapped sweets). Kids
will love the slimy texture, especially if they're blindfolded.

Stocking the Larder

As the summer months come to a close, it is time to think about stocking the larder for the short days and long winter months ahead. From chutneys and jams to preserves and pickles, a few homemade jars will cheer even the dreariest winter day.

CHUTNEY

Originating in India, the word chutney comes from the Hindu 'chatni'. It is made from fruits, vegetables, vinegar, sugar and spices. A smooth texture is achieved by cooking slowly for a long time, and an intense flavour develops when the mixture is left to mature for a few months.

Experts recommend that when making chutney, always chop by hand, and always chop the vegetables to the same size to ensure even cooking. Experiment with different combinations of fruit, vegetables and spices. Classic chutneys include apple, tomato and plum, and don't over look the mustardy-tang of piccalilli.

Store chutney in sterilised, sealed jars for up to a year. Leave the chutney to mature for about three months before eating – this allows the ingredients to absorb the vinegar and the vinegar to mellow. Freshly made chutneys can taste mouth-puckeringly harsh.

Chutneys are delicious as condiments, served with curries and roast meats. They perk up a plain cheese sandwich and can even be used to add flavour to casseroles.

Autumn Foraging

Blackberries: pick when deep purple–black

Hazelnuts: ready when leaves turn yellow

Mushrooms: seek advice on what's safe to eat

Rosehips: look out for them in hedgerows

Sloes: the fruit of the blackthorn tree — try making some delicious sloe gin

Wild garlic: wander through some woodland

JAM-MAKING TIPS

Use a preserving pan or large saucepan made of stainless steel. The fruit and sugar should only fill the pan to a third full. Dissolve the sugar on a low heat, before increasing to reach a rolling boil, to ensure it is properly dissolved and won't be crystallised in the jam. It is often recommended that some butter is added at the same time as the sugar to prevent any surface scum from forming.

Pectin is a natural setting agent that is found in fruit; the more acidic the fruit, the higher the pectin. Low-pectin fruit needs to be complemented by high-pectin fruit (or pectin-rich lemon juice, liquid pectin or jam sugar). High-pectin fruits include blackcurrants, damsons, gooseberries, lemons, oranges, plums and redcurrants. Raspberries have quite high pectin, whereas blackberries, elderberries, pears, strawberries, peaches and rhubarb are low in pectin.

Test whether your jam is set by putting a saucer in the freezer. Put a teaspoon of the hot jam on the cold saucer and push it with your finger – if it wrinkles, it is ready to set. If you have a jam thermometer the optimum temperature is 105°C.

Jars should be sterilised by washing in hot soapy water, then rinsing in clean warm water and leaving to drip-dry. Put the clean jars in the oven for half an hour at 140°C/Gas mark 1. Fill jars to the very top to allow for shrinkage, and cover with a wax disc, wax-side down, making sure there are no air bubbles trapped underneath. Cover the jars with their lids while they are still hot.

Freezing Fruit
Some fruits will freeze successfully for up to eight months.
Raspberries, blueberries and gooseberries: try open-freezing on a parchment-lined baking tray, and then transfer into a freezer container (e.g. an old ice cream tub).
Rhubarb can be dry frozen, sliced in freezer bags.
Apple should be sliced and blanched before freezing.

Classic Chutneys

Apple
Tomato
Plum
Piccalilli
Red onion

> "Simple well-made preserves – especially those of our early summer fruits – are most valuable domestic stores, as they will retain through the year or longer their peculiarly grateful and agreeable flavour."
>
> *Modern Cookery for Private Families, Eliza Acton*

Bonfire Night

Bonfire Night is the commemoration of a Catholic plot on 5 November 1605 to blow up the Houses of Parliament, using 36 barrels of gunpowder stored in a cellar under the House of Lords. That date has become enshrined in the English calendar – a time for bonfires and fireworks, and burning effigies of the notorious Catholic traitor and ringleader, Guy Fawkes.

Preparations for Bonfire Night celebrations include making a dummy of Guy Fawkes, 'the Guy'. Some children keep up an old tradition of walking in the streets, carrying their own homemade Guy, and begging passers-by for "a penny for the Guy". They use the money to buy fireworks for the evening festivities. On the night itself, the Guy is placed on top of the bonfire, which is then set alight and firework displays fill the sky.

The extent of the celebrations and the size of the bonfire varies from one community to the next. Lewes, in East Sussex, is famous for its Bonfire Night festivities, where the traditional Guy Fawkes figure is supplanted by an annual choice of topical effigy. The event consistently attracts thousands of people each year.

Many people feel inclined to leave the pyrotechnics to the professionals, restricting themselves – and their kids – to the comparatively tame pleasures of sparklers.

But if you're going to eschew the laid-on entertainment of professional displays, and feel inclined to recapture those thrilling November evenings of childhood, follow a few simple rules to ensure that the event is safe and doesn't upset your neighbours.

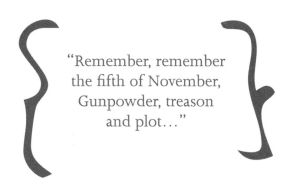

> "Remember, remember the fifth of November, Gunpowder, treason and plot…"

MULLED WINE

Put a bottle of red wine in a saucepan with one halved orange, 2oz/57g Demerara sugar, bay leaf, a cinnamon stick and some grated nutmeg. Heat gently until the sugar has dissolved. Taste to see if you want the wine sweeter, and add more sugar to taste. Once you have taken the pan off the heat stir in 2fl oz/60ml of damson or sloe gin. Strain into heatproof glasses and serve at once.

Tip: Prick the skin of large baking potatoes, rub in olive oil and wrap in tin foil. Place them in the embers of your bonfire and bake for at least an hour.

Top Tips for Bonfire Night

NEIGHBOURS

Remember that fireworks are noisy. Warn your neighbours – especially if they are pet-owners – and preferably invite them to firework parties. Be careful not to position bonfires upwind of neighbours' houses and don't let any pyromaniacs loose on the bonfire – you might end up with a bigger blaze than you bargained for.

SAFETY

Keep fireworks in a closed box until the party. Prepare fireworks carefully (e.g. nail the Catherine wheel to a tree, position the rockets in flowerbeds etc.) well before the guests arrive.
Ensure that there is a safe buffer zone between fireworks and guests, especially small children. Always light fireworks at arm's length and step back.

CHILDREN

Don't let children anywhere near fireworks or the bonfire. Lay on plenty of sparklers; they'll keep kids busy during hiatuses in the display – but do keep an eye on the kids and ensure that spent sparklers are disposed of quickly and safely; glowing sticks can pose a safety threat. Ensure your children are holding sparklers at arm's length.

TIMING

Keep the firework display contained to a certain timeframe (e.g. 7.30–8pm). Sporadic bursts punctuating the evening may irritate neighbours, disappoint guests and disrupt the flow of the evening. Remember, firework displays are soon over so make sure you've got food and drink ready for the immediate aftermath of the display.

An Autumn Supper Party

Autumn is the perfect season for entertaining. The long summer days are over and the nights are drawing in. As the weather outside deteriorates and the leaves fall, it's a pleasure to draw the curtains, light the fire and enjoy comfort food and good company.

This is the season when root vegetables come into their own. Parsnips can be roasted (add cumin or cardamom) and will add sweet richness to soups. Turnips and swedes both work well boiled, mashed (add plenty of butter) or roasted. Winter squash is also delicious roasted (add chilli and garlic) or will make an excellent soup.

Autumn is the season of the English apple. Make the most of seasonal Bramley apples and indulge in an autumnal apple crumble; you can make it different by adding cinnamon, almonds or blackerries. Serve with plenty of fresh custard.

Reflect the golds and russets of autumn in your table decorations.

Offset rich soups and casseroles with a lighter dessert: slice some apples and simmer gently with a cinnamon stick. When the sauce has thickened, serve it warm with vanilla ice cream or natural yoghurt.

Ensure that your dining room is draft-free and don't place guests too near the fire.

Opt for an autumnal theme in your table decorations: use seedheads, rosehips and autumn leaves, and add a touch of vibrant colour with seasonal flowers such as dahlias. Pick up the autumnal theme with yellow, orange and red tablecloths, napkins and candles.

Apples are a member of the rose family. The apple tree originated in an area between the Caspian and the Black Sea.

> "Around and around the house the leaves fall thick, but never fast, for they come circling down with a dead lightness that is sombre and slow."
>
> *Bleak House*, Charles Dickens

SQUASH SOUP

Cut a 1.5kg/3lb butternut squash into large chunks. Toss it in olive oil and roast it in an oven set at 190°C/gas mark 5 for 15–20 minutes. Meanwhile melt a mixture of butter and olive oil and gently 'sweat' an onion and a couple of leeks. Add the roasted squash, pour in 1.5 litres (2.75 pints) of chicken stock, season and simmer for 15 minutes before puréeing.

The richness of this soup is perfectly offset by a variety of herbs: try finishing off with chopped sage, rosemary or thyme.

BEEF CASSEROLE

2 onions, peeled and roughly chopped
3 carrots, peeled and roughly chopped
3 sticks of celery, trimmed and roughly chopped
4 cloves of garlic, unpeeled
2 sprigs of fresh rosemary
2 sprigs of thyme
2 bay leaves
1kg/2lb 3oz shin of beef, cut into 5cm/2in pieces
2 tins of plum tomatoes
half a bottle of robust red wine
salt and freshly ground black pepper

Heat your oven to 180°C/gas mark 4. In a heavy-bottomed ovenproof casserole dish, gently fry the onions, carrots, celery, garlic and herbs in olive oil for 5 minutes.

Toss the beef in seasoned flour and add to the pan. Gently fry until the meat is 'sealed' (browned), then add the tomatoes, wine and seasoning.

Gently bring to the boil, cover with a double-thickness piece of tin foil and a lid and place in your preheated oven for 3 hours.

Remove the thyme and rosemary and serve with buttery mashed potatoes (add swede or parsnip).

You can also add chopped root vegetables, such as turnips or parsnips, to the casserole an hour before serving.

Afternoon Tea

The quiet gentility of the English tea ceremony is seen as a reflection of the reserved national character. Your guests will enjoy the procession of delicious titbits, washed down by freshly brewed tea. This is an English ritual that is certainly worth preserving and treasuring.

It is said that Catherine of Braganza, the Portuguese wife of King Charles II, brought tea-drinking to England in the 1660s. For over a century its popularity did not match that of coffee. At first it was highly taxed and very expensive, only sold through apothecaries, coffee houses, snuff shops and through shops catering for ladies' needs.

The tradition of afternoon tea, when tea was served at 4pm with cakes, savouries and sweets, was started by the Duchess of Bedford in 1840 and has remained popular ever since. The evening meal in her household was served fashionably late at eight o'clock, thus leaving a long period of time between lunch and dinner. The Duchess would become hungry around four o'clock in the afternoon and asked that a tray of tea, bread and butter, and cake be brought to her room during the late afternoon. This became a habit of hers and she began inviting friends to join her.

This pause for tea became a fashionable social event. During the 1880s, upper-class and society women would change into long gowns, gloves and hats for their afternoon tea which was usually served in the drawing room between four and five o'clock.

{ "There are few hours in life more agreeable than the hour dedicated to the ceremony known as afternoon tea." }

Henry James

Serve tea in china teacups, with saucers and teaspoons. Provide side plates for food.

Perfect Scones

The National Trust provides thousands of scones for hungry visitors every day. This is their recommended recipe (makes 12):

350g/12oz self-raising flour, sifted
50g/1.8 oz butter, softened
50g/1.8 oz lard, softened
100-115ml/3.5-4fl oz milk

Cakes for Afternoon Tea

Dundee cake
Madeira cake (zested lemon)
Victoria sponge sandwich
Chocolate cake
Lemon cake with clotted cream

One night in 1762 John Montagu, the 4th Earl of Sandwich, was too busy gambling to stop for a meal. It is said that he ordered a waiter to bring him roast beef between two slices of bread, so he wouldn't get his fingers greasy while eating the meal. The sandwich was born.

A TRADITIONAL AFTERNOON TEA

If you're entertaining friends for a proper afternoon tea, you should supply a selection of dainty sandwiches (crusts removed), assorted cakes and pastries and scones served with clotted cream and preserves. Traditionally, the Devon method of serving cream tea is to split the scone in two, cover each half with clotted cream, and then add strawberry jam on top. In Cornwall, the scone is first spread with strawberry jam, with the cream added as the topping. Many people will find the Cornish method an easier way to handle the clotted cream.

Savouries are eaten first, followed by scones, then cakes. Smaller cakes will look impressive arranged on a decorative cake stand. Pile it high with butterfly cakes, cupcakes, chocolate mini muffins and jam tarts.

Preheat the oven to 190°C/ gas mark 5. Grease two baking trays. Rub the fats into the flour, working as quickly and lightly as possible with cold hands. Add enough milk to give a soft, bread-like dough. On a floured board, roll out to a thickness of 1.5cm/0.6in and cut into rounds with 6cm/2.4in cutter. Place on the prepared trays and bake for 15-20 minutes until lightly golden and well risen. Remove from the oven and lift on to a wire rack to cool.

Sandwiches for Afternoon Tea

Thinly sliced cucumber
Smoked salmon
Finely sliced ham, mustard optional
Egg mayonnaise with chopped chives

A Refreshing Cuppa

In Britain tea is seen as a universal panacea for all ills, and the British love nothing better than 'putting their feet up' and enjoying a 'cuppa'. For many of us, everyday tea comes in a teabag. But understanding your tea and experimenting with various blends will be extremely rewarding.

SERVING TEA

If serving tea for a group it is worth brewing a pot. Loose leaf tea will taste best. A second pot with hot water in it should be provided in order to dilute over-brewed tea if necessary. Use one rounded teaspoon of tea per cup and leave it to brew for 2–4 minutes before pouring. Use water that has boiled, but is not actually boiling.

When stirring the tea don't clink the spoon against your cup.

If a waiter places a teapot on the table without pouring the tea the person nearest the pot should pour for everyone. The tea should be poured first (through a strainer if the tea is loose-leaf), and any milk, lemon or sugar added afterwards. Once you have stirred your tea remove the spoon from the cup and place it on the saucer. In Victorian times hot tea was poured straight into the cup to test the quality of the bone china. Expensive china did not crack.

Don't put milk or lemon in the cup before you pour the tea.

When serving lemon with tea, place a slice (not chunk) of lemon in the cup after it has been poured. Never add milk to lemon tea; the citric acid in the lemon will make the milk curdle.

Don't overfill your cup so that tea slops into the saucer and place the cup back on the saucer between sips. Hold the handle of the teacup between your thumb and forefinger, don't hold your little finger in the air. Don't dunk your biscuits in your tea unless in a very informal setting, and don't make slurping noises – even if it is hot.

If seated at the table never lift your saucer up as you raise your cup.

A Tea-Drinker's Guide

TEA ESSENTIALS

After plucking, the fresh leaves of *Camellia sinensis* are spread out to dry. Then the leaves are either rolled to crush the leaf and release the essential oils and enzymes, or passed through a 'cut, tear and curl' machine. After that the tea is left to ferment until it becomes a bright copper colour. Then it's dried to halt the fermentation and sterilise the leaves.

GREEN TEA

Immediately after plucking, the leaves are softened by steaming in large iron pans over a fire. They are then rolled and dried, but are not fermented.

BLACK TEA

Black tea is the most popular variety of tea drunk in the UK and is more oxidized than the oolong and green varieties. After plucking and drying, the leaves are then rolled out so that the mix of warm air, aromatic juices, bacteria and enzymes leads to oxidation (this fermentation is a natural reaction that affects strength and colour). Fermentation is stopped by 'firing' the leaves with hot air, which makes them turn black as they dry. Assam, English Breakfast, Kenya, Earl Grey, Lapsang Souchong and Darjeeling (the "Champagne of teas") are all black teas.

OOLONG TEA

Means 'black dragon' in Chinese and is traditionally used for a tea that is semi-fermented. After plucking, oolong teas are processed in a similar way to black teas, but the fermentation time is much shorter. They tend to have a large leaf and produce a pale bright liquor with a delicate flavour.

HERBAL TEAS

Herbal infusions are made from the fruits, flowers, leaves, seeds or roots of a variety of plants, which are then boiled and strained. Popular herbal teas include: camomile, Moroccan mint, peppermint, ginger, lemon balm, cardamon.

WHITE TEA

This tea is unfermented; only the unopened bud and sometimes the first new leaf are used.

BLEND YOUR OWN

If you want to make your own unique blend, sample as many varieties as possible and make notes on leaf colour, fragrance and taste. Then experiment with combining two different tea types: you might, for example, want to add a small amount of fragrant lapsang souchong to a more robust Darjeeling. Once you've made a great blend, make up a caddy-full, keep it airtight and note down the quantities you've used.

A Sunday Roast

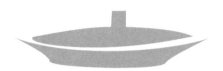

For most British people a Sunday lunch is synonymous with roast meat, roast potatoes, gravy and vegetables. So embrace the tradition and enjoy sharing this delicious meal with friends and family.

The British are well known as avid consumers of roast beef, so much so that the French have dubbed them 'rosbifs'. The consumption of roast beef became an almost patriotic pastime, part of British cultural identity. In 1748, when the artist William Hogarth was arrested in Calais, he painted 'The Roast Beef of Old England', a mouth-watering paeon of praise to Anglo-Saxon food, set in sterling opposition to a French dish of soup.

When the French traveller Henri Misson de Valbourg visited London in 1698 he recounted how "it is a common practice, even among People of Good Substance, to have a huge Piece of Roast-Beef on Sundays, of which they stuff until they can swallow no more, and eat the rest cold, without any other Victuals, the other six Days of the Week."

Poorer people, who did not have a large fireplace, would drop off a smaller joint at the baker's on their way to church. Bread was not baked on a Sunday (the day of rest) so meat could be cooked in the cooling bread ovens – thus the tradition of Sunday lunch for all was established.

A Sunday roast is a perfect entertaining opportunity. If you source good meat, perfect the art of making roast potatoes and gravy, and provide a range of in-season vegetables and a traditional sauce to accompany the meat, your meals will prove enduringly popular. The Sunday lunch will turn into a lazy, drawn-out all-afternoon affair, and well-fed guests will find it hard to drag themselves away.

If you've got some vegetarians on your guest list, try and accommodate them with an easily prepared dish. For example you could sauté some leeks and thyme in butter, place them on ready-made puff pastry and add a topping of goat's cheese. Cook the tart for 25 minutes at 220°C/gas mark 7 (you could put it on the top shelf while your roast potatoes are cooking and your roast meat is resting).

MEAT ROASTING TIMES

BEEF: initial 20 mins at 220°C/gas mark 7, then 10–15 minutes per 450g/1lb at 190°C/gas mark 6 (rare), 20 mins per 450g/1lb (medium) and 25 minutes per 450g/1lb (well-done). Rest for 30 minutes.

LAMB: initial 20 mins at 220°C/gas mark 7, then 20 mins per 450g/1lb at 190°C/gas mark 5. Allow the meat to rest for 30 minutes before carving.

PORK: initial 20 mins at 220°C/gas mark 7, then 35 mins per 450g at 190°C/gas mark 5. Check the juices run clear and rest for 30 minutes.

CHICKEN: 20 mins per 450g/1lb at 190°C/gas mark 5, plus 20 minutes extra. Most small birds take under an hour: turn the heat up to 220°C/gas mark 7 for the final fifteen minutes to crisp off the skin. It is essential to check that the juices run clear. Rest for 30 minutes.

These are guidelines: the timings will depend on the efficiency of your oven, as well as the temperature of the meat when you start.

Homemade Sauces

HORSERADISH SAUCE FOR BEEF
100g/3½oz horseradish root
150ml/¼ pint double cream
1 tsp sugar
½ tsp yellow mustard powder
2 tsp white wine vinegar
salt and pepper

Soak the horseradish root for an hour, then wash, scrape clean
and grate. Whip the cream. Fold the grated horseradish into
the cream and add sugar, mustard, salt, pepper and vinegar.
Chill in the fridge for at least 2 hours.

MINT SAUCE FOR LAMB
bunch of mint
4 tbsp boiling water
4 tbsp white wine vinegar
1 level tbsp caster sugar

Strip off the mint leaves, sprinkle with salt and chop finely.
Place in a jug, add the sugar and boiling water, stir and
leave to cool. Stir in the vinegar and sugar and adjust the
seasoning as necessary.

APPLE SAUCE FOR PORK
900g/2lbs Bramley cooking apples, peeled, cored and sliced
4–5 tbsp cold water
juice of ½ lemon
1 tbsp caster sugar
50g/2oz unsalted butter, cut into cubes

Place the sliced apple in a saucepan with the water and lemon
juice. Cook over low heat, stirring occasionally for about 12–
15 minutes until the apples have softened. Stir in the sugar
and whisk in the cubes of butter and keep warm.

*Note: Whisk a knob of butter into your gravy for a
glossy finish*

Stir-Up Sunday, Canapés, Christmas Presents, Good Games, Turkey Curry

Hogmanay, New Year's Eve, Burns Night, Valentine's Day, Shrove Tuesday

December 21st – March 21st

It may be cold outside, but winter is a peak season for home entertaining. There is the long, enjoyable build-up to Christmas – an extravaganza of home baking, present-buying and festive decorating. And after all the champagne and feasting on the big day there are further celebrations to come – Hogmanay and Burns Night, with their ancient customs and traditional foods such as cock-a-leekie soup and haggis. Valentine's Day punctuates the long, dreary days of mid-winter, a perfect excuse for tempting delicacies, and Pancake Day, and spring, is not far behind.

The Best of Winter

With frosty mornings, shorter days and usually a dusting of snow, seasonal winter produce often seems sparse. However, there are many treats in store as root vegetables are in abundance, game is still readily available and many fish are at their best.

WINTER TREAT: SEVILLE ORANGES
January sees the brief season of Seville oranges, the prized, bittersweet Spanish fruits that make the best marmalade. The oranges freeze well, so stock up now and you will be well-prepared for marmalade-making later in the year.

WINTER TIP: THE PERFECT JACKET POTATO
Choose a floury variety, such as King Edward, Maris Piper or Marfona. Wash well, and prick a few times with a fork. Rub a little olive oil into the skin, and then some sea salt (the oil should help it stick). Place directly onto the oven shelf and bake at 180–200°C/Gas mark 4–6 for 1–1.5 hours. Serve with plenty of butter.

WINTER HIGHLIGHT: OYSTERS
Oysters are best eaten in winter months when waters are at their coldest. Live, unopened oysters should be stored in the fridge, covered by a wet tea towel (never in water or an airtight container). Some of the most prized British oysters are from Whitstable in Kent, Colchester in Essex and the Helford River in Cornwall.

Seasonal Produce
Black bream
Brussels sprouts
Cabbage
Carrots
Celeriac
Chicory
Duck
Endive
Goose
Guinea fowl
Halibut
Hare
Leeks
Monkfish
Mussels

SEASONAL VASE
Amaryllis
Dogwood
Narcissi
Pussy Willow

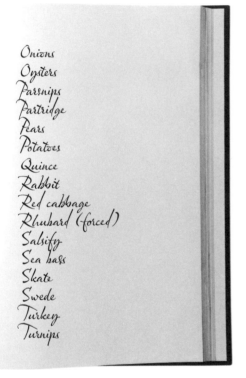

Onions
Oysters
Parsnips
Partridge
Pears
Potatoes
Quince
Rabbit
Red cabbage
Rhubarb (forced)
Salsify
Sea bass
Skate
Swede
Turkey
Turnips

SEASONAL SPECIALS

Aromatic, yellow-skinned, seasonal QUINCES are most famous as an accompaniment to Spanish cheese in the form of a paste, called membrillo. As well as a tangy addition to the cheese board, a quince paste makes a wonderful coating for roast ham.

As an alternative to the usual winter root vegetables, keep an eye out for SALSIFY. Also known as the oyster plant, these long, thin, brown roots have a cream-coloured flesh. Try roasting them with a little garlic, or boiling and then sautéeing them.

Another seasonal root vegetable to enjoy is SWEDE. Known as 'neeps' in Scotland and as 'rutabaga' in America, swede is a member of the cabbage family. The skin is thick and tough, but the flesh is sweet and tender when cooked. Try them boiled and mashed (with butter and black pepper) or simply roasted.

From January, forced RHUBARB is readily available. Grown in the dark, the stems have a distinctive crimson-pink colour, and the leaves are a yellowy-green (rhubarb leaves are poisonous). Forced rhubarb is sweeter than the field-grown stems that are in season later in the year, and it is also more delicate. Try it poached or baked, paired with ginger or vanilla.

Christmas Preparation

Even with the best planning and preparation, the weeks before Christmas are always unavoidably busy with shopping, cooking and socialising. It is, therefore, sensible to turn your attention to the mixing bowl well in advance, ideally in late November on Stir-Up Sunday. This will give your Christmas pudding and Christmas cake plenty of time to mellow and mature.

"Stir up, we beseech thee, O Lord, the wills of thy faithful people..."

The phrase Stir-Up Sunday originates from the collect in the Book of Common Prayer that was read on the last Sunday before Advent. It is said that church-goers heard the words "Stir up, we beseech thee…" and were inspired to get started on making their Christmas puddings.

Everyone in the family would take a turn to stir the Christmas pudding mixture, with the youngest child going first, always stirring from east to west in honour of the Magi. Charms were also included in the mixture, the most popular being a silver coin that would signify a year of wealth to the lucky recipient.

By making Christmas pudding this far in advance, the mixture is given plenty of time to intensify in flavour and develop a more compact texture. By Christmas Day, the pudding will have matured to become sweet, rich, moist and mellow.

"Mrs. Cratchit entered – flushed, but smiling proudly – with the pudding, like a speckled cannon-ball, so hard and firm, blazing in half of half-a-quarter of ignited brandy, and bedight with Christmas holly stuck into the top."

A Christmas Carol, Charles Dickens

PANETTONE
Try something different and opt for a Christmas Panettone – sweet fruit bread originating from Milan. It is baked in special moulds to give it a unique tubular shape, and is served in slices, like a loaf of bread, traditionally accompanied by a hot sweet drink or sweet wine.

STOLLEN
This German Christmas cake, originating from Dresden, is a light fruitcake with a bread-like texture, filled with marzipan and studded with dried fruit. It is topped with sugar or a glace icing, and is a good alternative for those who find Christmas cake too heavy.

Christmas Cake Tips

Christmas cake should be rich, spicy, moist, fruity and boozy. Look out for recipes that include interesting fruits such as blueberries, dates, cranberries, golden sultanas and dried figs.

Soak the fruit overnight to ensure it is plump – try brandy, rum, whisky or sherry. If you are pushed for time, try to soak it for at least a few hours.

Follow the recipe and timings carefully, and always make sure that your oven is properly pre-heated to the correct temperature before you put in the cake.

Always double-line the cake tin with baking parchment. If the top of the cake starts to brown too quickly, protect it with a piece of baking parchment.

You will know that the cake is cooked when a skewer, inserted into the middle of the cake, comes out clean. Leave the cake in its baking parchment when it comes out of the oven.

Allow to cool for about half an hour, and then turn it upside down to finish cooling. This will give you a satisfyingly flat-topped cake to ice and decorate.

Poke a few holes into the underside of the cake. Feed it weekly with a spirit of your choice – brandy is always a favourite – until you come to ice it nearer Christmas.

Opt for traditional royal icing with an underlayer of homemade marzipan and apricot jam. Smooth the icing with a ruler, or create little soft peaks. Decorate creatively.

Traditional Christmas Decorations

Every year we dust off boxes of decorations, check the Christmas tree lights and head out into the crisp air to cut sprigs of holly. Many of our traditions date back hundreds of years, yet others are surprisingly recent.

It's beginning to look a lot like Christmas...

Christmas trees were first popularised in Great Britain by Queen Victoria and Prince Albert. In 1848, the *Illustrated London News* depicted the Queen and her family around their Christmas tree, and a new trend caught on. Christmas trees were already popular in parts of Europe, especially Germany (Prince Albert's homeland), but soon households across the country were adorning fir trees with candles, small presents, sweets and fruits.

Deck the hall with boughs of holly... Tis the season to be jolly.

Houses have been decorated with winter foliage – holly, ivy, bay and rosemary – as far back as medieval times, as the evergreen nature of the plants represented everlasting life. The prickly holly leaves were also said to drive evil spirits away, but later it was considered bad luck to have holly in the house before Christmas Eve. Christmas poinsettias can be traced back to a 16th-century Mexican legend, with the red star-shaped leaves representing the Star of Bethlehem and the Crucifixion.

Chestnuts roasting on an open fire, Jack Frost nipping at your nose...

The tradition of the Yule log began in Britain in the 1700s. On Christmas Eve, a large, heavy log (sometimes even a tree that filled most of a room) would be selected and decorated with ribbons, before being dragged into the hearth. It was then lit with a torch made of wood from the previous year's Yule log, and kept alight for the twelve days of Christmas. After Twelfth Night, the Yule log's ashes was scattered on the land, as they were believed to bring fertility to the soil.

On the twelfth day of Christmas, my true love gave to me...

The evening of the fifth of January, also the eve of the Epiphany, is commonly recognised as Twelfth Night. It is seen as bad luck to have Christmas decorations hung up past this point. Twelfth Night therefore provides a good deadline for getting the decorations put away and the bulk of the thank you letters written.

Christmas Eve Drinks Party

With days of festivities ahead, a Christmas Eve drinks party should all be about elegant simplicity. The party spirit should come easily as guests have finally finished work for the Christmas break, and children are gripped with excitement and anticipation about what Christmas (and Father Christmas) will bring.

Forward planning is key – don't overload yourself (or your guests) before the main festivities have begun. The best Christmas eves are ones that feel relaxed and informal, so keep it easy. Canapés should be plentiful, but choose ones that can be made in advance and don't require last minute cooking or garnishing.

Opt for timeless, classic and elegant drinks. Avoid the expected mulled wine and supplement the staples – i.e. beer and wine – with a couple of classic cocktails to add sense of occasion. It goes without saying that drivers and non-drinkers should also be catered for.

Champagne Cocktail

Ingredients
1 white sugar cube
2 dashes Angostura bitters
20 ml/0.7 fl oz Cognac
Champagne (chilled)

Method
On a spoon, soak the sugar cube with the bitters and then drop into the bottom of a champagne flute. Add the Cognac, and top up with champagne. Serve immediately.

Classic Nibbles

Cocktail sausages
Cheese straws
Mini sausage rolls
Soft-boiled quail eggs
Olives

Traditionally, mistletoe represented good luck, health and fertility, and kissing under the mistletoe was seen to encourage marriage. Why not hang a bunch up to encourage some Christmas romance?

Manhattan
Ingredients
40ml/1.5fl oz rye whiskey
20ml/0.7fl oz Italian vermouth
Dash Angostura bitters
1 maraschino cherry

Method
Stir in a mixing glass and then strain into a v-shaped cocktail glass. Garnish with the maraschino cherry. Serve immediately.

CANAPÉ RULES

- Keep it to just one mouthful – biting a canapé in two is a tricky business.

- Keep the presentation sleek by serving just one type of canapé per serving plate.

- Provide some empty dishes so skewers and cocktail sticks can be deposited.

- Don't overstretch yourself: make sure you have a mix of simple nibbles and more complex canapés.

- If you're aiming to fill people up, provide plenty of bread-based options (bruschetta, crostini etc.).

- Add a luxurious festive touch to your canapés and drinks by garnishing them with edible gold leaf.

> "Twas the Night Before Christmas,
> when all through the house
> Not a creature was stirring, not even a mouse.
> The stockings were hung by the chimney with care,
> In hopes that St Nicholas soon would be there."
>
> *Twas the night before Christmas, Clement Clarke Moore*

Christmas Day Lunch

Christmas lunch is often the biggest and busiest meal we cook all year. With numerous trimmings, timings and traditions to uphold, it can become a stressful and daunting prospect. Good preparation and organisation are essential.

PLANNING THE TIME

Draw up a timing plan by first calculating the cooking time of the turkey (or meat of choice), and then working out how everything else will fit in. Another crucial starting point is the time lunch will be served – once that is decided, you can work out when things need to go into the oven. You can also plan what hobs you will need to use.

TURKEY TIMINGS

A turkey should be roasted from room temperature, in a properly preheated oven. Cooking times vary according to the oven, but as a general rule allow 30–40 minutes per kilogram, plus an extra 20–30 minutes if the bird is stuffed. Remove the wishbone before roasting to make carving easier.

Roast the bird for the first 30–40 minutes at approximately 220°C/gas mark 7, then turn the oven down to 170°C/gas mark 3 for the remaining cooking time. Alternatively, just cook for 20 minutes per 500g at 180°C/gas mark 4 for the whole cooking time.

Baste the bird every 20 minutes, and cover with foil to keep it moist. Remove the foil for the last 40 minutes of cooking time to brown the skin. Check the turkey is cooked by inserting a skewer into the thickest part of the leg – the juices should run clear.

PERFECT ROASTIES

Use a floury potato such as Maris Piper. Parboil, and then add to a roasting tray of hot goose fat. Ensure each potato is evenly covered, and roast for 30–40 minutes in a preheated oven at 180°C/gas mark 4. Turn occasionally to make sure they are evenly browned. If they are not quite done when the meat comes out to rest, turn the oven up to 220°C/gas mark 7 to crisp them up.

CHRISTMAS EVE PREP

Christmas Eve is the perfect time to get as much ready as possible before the mayhem of guests, presents, bucks fizz and hot, busy kitchens on the big day.

- Prep as much as possible in advance – spuds, Brussels sprouts, parsnips, carrots, crumbs for the bread sauce, brandy butter...

- If you are eating in the dining room, lay the table. This will give you extra time on Christmas morning in case there are last-minute problems.

- Chill the white wine and champagne – polish glasses and flutes.

- Count out all the china and serving dishes. Allocate saucepans and baking trays. Think about post-lunch coffee and have cups and saucers ready.

- Double check you bought all the ingredients, sauces and trimmings you need. Ensure you have a plentiful supply of tin foil.

- Last thing before bed, take the turkey out of the fridge. This will ensure it is cooking from room temperature the following day and will mean your timings will be accurate.

- Leave out a brandy for Father Christmas, and have one yourself...

SAGE & ONION STUFFING

Combine finely chopped fresh sage and onion with fresh white breadcrumbs, and bind with beaten egg. Roll into small balls and bake till golden brown. There are many variations to this classic accompaniment, including the addition of lemon zest, pork mincemeat and offal, namely liver.

LUNCH THROUGH THE AGES

In medieval England, Christmas lunch was either peacock or boar. Henry VIII is credited as being the first English monarch to opt for a festive turkey, and it soon became a fashionable choice. Until Victorian times, however, it was equally popular to eat goose.

"We can hardly imagine an object of greater envy than is presented by a respected portly pater-familias carving, at the season devoted to good cheer and genial charity, his own fat turkey, and carving it well. The only art consists, as in the carving of a goose, in getting from the breast as many fine slices as possible."

Mrs Beeton's Book of Household Management

Christmas Manners

The festive season all too often strains good manners to the limit. Expectations for this much-hyped 'special day' are high, but the claustrophobia of family get-togethers can easily lead to tension, cross words and disharmony. Plan ahead carefully to avoid these common pitfalls.

If you're the Christmas host, then you will find you have a big juggling act on your hands. You may well be dealing with several different generations, as well as bringing together representatives of two entirely separate families (united by marriage). All that, and presents and food too!

Make your guests feel involved in planning the structure of the day.

Difficulties frequently arise when two different families unite for Christmas celebrations. The tendency to fetishise your own family's version of Christmas ("We always go to midnight mass and open our presents before lunch etc. etc.") can make new arrivals feel dragooned into your own family mythology. So, make tentative suggestions ("we normally open our presents before lunch – is that ok with you?") rather than confident pronouncements.

Never presume everyone will be captivated by your over-excited children.

Grandparents, however doting, will soon wilt if they are forced to spend hours in an overcrowded sitting room watching children play havoc with their Christmas booty. Provide a quiet zone where the older, less hyper-active, guests can retreat for drinks and civilised conversation.

Don't inflict agonisingly long meals on small children.

Do your best to accommodate the excitement of the children, and remember grumpiness is not an option at this special time of year. If you've room, try and head the children off into a different part of the house. If possible take them on a walk or let them play in the garden.

Indulge your children's desire to play with their presents. It's much better to enjoy adult company and conversation than to find yourself sitting at a table feeling frazzled by unhappy kids.

Good Games for Christmas

Monopoly
Trivial Pursuit
Scrabble
Cluedo
Pass the Bomb
Blokus
Jenga
Parcheesi

If you are in the panic-stricken last stages of preparation for the Christmas lunch, and desperate for someone to do some pre-emptive washing up or tidying away, don't hesitate to ask. Guests will leap to their feet when help is solicited, because they feel guilty when they're lounging around not doing anything.

Always ask for help when you need it.

Don't demand too much of yourself, your family or your guests. Building up your expectations of the day to dizzy heights will mean that mishaps and misunderstandings (however minor) are blown up out of all proportion – and that's not what Christmas is about.

Don't expect perfection.

> "A lovely thing about Christmas is that it's compulsory, like a thunderstorm, and we all go through it together."
> Garrison Keillor

GOLDEN RULES FOR A GREAT CHRISTMAS

- Write down a cooking timetable and stick to it.

- Lay on generous supplies of champagne (or similar). Glasses can be dispensed throughout the day when spirits are flagging.

- Pace the day. Spread out the main events (present-opening, lunch, games, TV) to ensure there aren't too many hiatuses.

- Buy plenty of batteries!

- Make sure you've got plenty of board games and some packs of cards.

- Plan television viewing ahead and record programmes to avoid clashes and ensure that family viewing is not steam-rollered by one interest group.

- Create quiet spaces where guests can take time out from the festivities.

Christmas Presents

It's Christmas morning; confronted by the book you've already read, the clothes you will never wear, the perfume that smells like disinfectant and the socks you don't need, you must call on all your powers of dissembling. You must never, ever look anything but delighted with your present.

Lack of taste is regrettable, but not a criminal offence.

Never allow yourself to become stuck in a competitive giving campaign. If someone showers you with extravagant presents you are not under a moral obligation to reciprocate, or outdo them. Take a firm stand, and stop the madness. It may dissipate the magic, but explicit negotiations (e.g. agreeing an upper spending limit) can save you from Christmas Day trauma.

Costly presents may detonate waves of guilt, obligation and social embarrassment.

Give yourself plenty of time to shop, and avoid any last-minute frenzy. Crowded stores and clocks ticking towards closing time lead to panic, unwarranted extravagance and terrible errors of judgement. If the whole present-buying experience turns sour, don't take out your frustration on the innocent recipient, thrusting the gift at them with bad grace.

Grumpy giving will never elicit true gratitude, and rightly so.

Re-gifting is a potential minefield. Certainly, as the credit-crunch bites, recycling is to be applauded, but employ great caution. Inspect presents minutely to ensure that there are no telltale signs that they are second-hand. Then think very carefully about who gave them to you in the first place; there is a very real possibility that you will re-gift a present to the original giver, or to someone who is intimately connected with them – this is a *faux pas* from which it is hard to recover.

Boasting about your re-gifting will make friends feel nervous about your presents.

Finally, be prepared. Buy a few generic presents (alcohol, chocolates, toiletries), wrap them, and keep them to hand. With this mini-arsenal, you will be admirably well-equipped to deal with everyone's Christmas nightmare: the surprise present…

Thank You Letters

The art of letter-writing may eventually be supplanted by the email or text message, but it is far from dead. In a digital age a handwritten thank you note will always look spontaneous and heart-felt, and is infinitely preferable to an email, text message or phone call.

Always write a thank you letter promptly, and at the latest by Twelfth Night (5th January). Ensure that you refer specifically to the present at the outset, and make a positive comment about it ("Thank you so much for the maroon gloves; they will go perfectly with my new handbag"). Add a little news about your own Christmas, and make polite enquiries about the recipient's, then reiterate your thanks and good wishes.

CHILDREN'S THANK YOUS

Write thank you letters on the behalf of small children. As soon as they are old enough to write, make sure they write their own.

Children should be encouraged to write thank you letters to people who have sent them presents (it is not necessary if they opened the present in front of the giver). They should specifically refer to the present in the letter, and make a detailed comment about it ("Thank you for the teddy you gave me for Christmas. I have named him Edward"). An extra sentence of topical news about the child's life adds a personal touch ("On Boxing Day Mummy and Daddy took me to see Cinderella").

Boxing Day

After a tiring and indulgent Christmas Day, Boxing Day provides the chance to enjoy a low-key get-together with friends and family. Keep the food simple, the style informal and the timings relaxed. Sometimes, it's the easy-going gatherings that are the most memorable Christmas occasions…

Hosts should revive jaded guests with plenty of drinks and nibbles.

The thought of another social gathering can sometimes be too much to bear for both hosts and guests. Over-indulgence on Christmas Day can result in tender heads and tummies, so hosts should aim to provide a relaxed and easy-going environment. Provide plenty of pre-lunch drinks to perk everyone up – champagne is the ultimate reviver, but also stock up on lager, bitter and wine, plenty of sparkling water and soft drinks. Keep the nibbles simple and tasty with bowls of crisps, nuts, olives etc.

After the formalities of Christmas Day, opt for casual dining or a buffet.

Lunch should be a casual affair, with the most obvious and traditional choice being turkey curry. It is quick and easy to make, and is kind on the washing up. Don't attempt to seat large groups of people – if you are hosting more guests than your dining table comfortably seats, then opt for a buffet. Bring out the Christmas Day leftovers and leave people to dig in as they please – guests will find the informality a refreshing change after the marathon of Christmas lunch.

Give nannies, cleaners, babysitters, postman and milkmen a festive tip.

Although it is a public holiday in many countries, the term 'Boxing Day' is used in the UK, Australia, Canada, New Zealand and some Commonwealth countries. The name is said to derive from when many households used to give their staff a day off on Boxing Day as a reward for having worked on Christmas Day. The servants used to be given a box of supplies – presents, a Christmas bonus, festive leftovers – to take home to their families. Tradesmen also used to do their rounds on the first weekday after Christmas Day, collecting a box of presents or money, similar to a Christmas bonus.

A Classic Leftover Turkey Curry

Serves 4

1 tbsp olive oil
25g/1oz unsalted butter
2 meduim onions, peeled and finely chopped
3 garlic cloves, peeled and finely chopped
Small knob of fresh ginger (about 2–3cm),
     peeled and finely chopped
8 green cardamom pods, lightly crushed to open
1 tsp ground coriander
2 tsp ground cumin
0.5 tsp chilli powder
1 tbsp ground turmeric
1 tsp garam masala
4 large tomatoes, chopped
800g/1lb 12oz leftover roasted turkey, chopped into small pieces
125ml/4fl oz natural yoghurt
4 tbsp crème fraîche
1 tbsp fresh lemon juice
1 tbsp fresh coriander leaves, chopped

1. Heat the oil and butter in a deep frying pan or casserole pot. Add the onions and cook over a medium heat until softened.

2. Add the garlic, ginger, cardamom, ground coriander, ground cumin, chilli powder, ground turmeric and garam masala, and fry for a few seconds until fragrant.

3. Add the chopped tomatoes and mix well to ensure the spices aren't stuck to the bottom of the pan.

4. Gently stir in the turkey and simmer for a few minutes to cook through. Season with salt and freshly ground black pepper.

5. Stir in the yoghurt, then add the crème fraîche and lemon juice. Recheck the seasoning.

6. Garnish with the chopped fresh coriander leaves, and serve immediately with steamed rice.

Note: Don't forget to serve the traditional accompaniments: poppadoms, mango chutney and lime pickle...

Hogmanay

Dating back to pagan celebrations of the Winter Solstice, the New Year's Eve festival of Hogmanay, enjoyed all over Scotland, is the perfect excuse for a party wherever you are. Incorporate some ancient traditions in your celebrations and enjoy reviving the superstitions of the past.

A CLEAN SLATE

It's considered unlucky to welcome in the New Year in an uncleaned house, so use Hogmanay as the spur to get out your dusters and mops and give your house a good spring-clean – it will probably need it after the prolonged Christmas festivities.

In Scotland cleaning the house is called 'redding', getting ready for the New Year.

EVERGREEN ENCHANTMENTS

Branches of rowan, placed over the doorway, are said to bring good luck. Mistletoe is believed to bring good health (not kisses) to the household. Pieces of holly are said to deter mischievous fairies, while hazel and yew are believed to protect the house and all who live in it. Juniper, burnt in all the grates, fills the house with a pungent scent, and doors and windows are flung open to let in the fresh air, ready for the celebrations.

Fill your tallest vase with a striking arrangement of symbolic greenery.

ON THE MIDNIGHT HOUR

As the bells ring in the New Year, link arms and sing Auld Lang Syne (which means 'A Long Time Ago'). Once people have finished singing, it's time to raise glasses, and toast the New Year.

FIRST-FOOTING

As soon as the bells have rung people go out to visit friends and family, bearing a bottle of warming spirits (usually whisky) for the New Year dram. Traditionally, the first-footer was a tall, dark haired man (women and redheads were considered unlucky). It was considered quite acceptable to turn away an 'unlucky' first-footer, or someone who knocked at the door empty-handed.

CAKE DAY

As well as being called Hogmanay in Scotland, New Year's Eve used to be known as Cake Day. This was because people would go out guising (dressing up) from door to door to get a piece of cake from their neighbours. It is still called Cake Day by some Scottish people and those from the North of England.

RESOLUTIONS

The Roman celebration of New Year was centred on the two-headed Roman god Janus, who looked both forward and back. Many Romans looked for forgiveness from their enemies and also exchanged gifts before the beginning of each year. This is thought to be the origin of the New Year's resolution – a belief that past evil spirits, entities or demons were banished when frailties, temptations, bad habits, and past transgressions were denounced.

FIRST-FOOTERS SHOULD CARRY THE FOLLOWING GIFTS:

A bottle of spirits
(for the New Year's toast)

A lump of coal
(to bring comfort for the following year)

A black bun, or shortbread
(to indicate the household won't go hungry)

A silver coin
(to signify prosperity)

Never go first-footing empty-handed

A New Year's Eve Celebration

Clean the house, light the fires, make some seasonal foods, and make sure you have plenty of warming liquor. You're all set for a traditional New Year's Eve celebration…

A New Year's Spread

Be prepared to greet and refresh your first footers with some traditional Scottish hospitality:

BLACK BUN

Made several weeks before Hogmanay, the black bun is a rich concoction of flour, brown sugar, currants, raisins, sultanas, almonds, ginger, cinnamon, cayenne pepper, mixed spice, whisky or brandy, buttermilk and eggs. This mixture is then wholly encased in pastry and baked in the oven.

SCOTCH BROTH SOUP

A hearty, warming soup for New Year's day (or night), made of neck (or breast) of lamb or mutton, pearl barley, onion, leeks, swedes, carrots, potatoes and chopped cabbage.

CLOOTIE DUMPLING

Round off your meal with this pudding, made of suet, oatmeal, sultanas, currants, golden syrup, sugar and eggs. The mixture is wrapped in a cloth and steamed for three hours.

SHORTBREAD

Good at any time of the year, but much baked around Hogmanay, Scottish shortbread is a mixture of plain and self-raising flour, butter, caster sugar and a pinch of salt. The butter and sugar are creamed together before combining with the sieved flour. The mixture is hand-shaped, never rolled, and is baked for an hour in a very low oven.

A WEE DRAM

Whisky should be drunk however you like it best; adding water to a single malt is no longer frowned upon by the cognoscenti.

Diluting blended whisky with soft drinks, such as lemonade or ginger ale, is also acceptable.

Whisky is best imbibed from a heavy-based glass, often crystal, to capture and concentrate the intense, peaty aroma.

A HET PINT

This winter-warmer was a traditional tipple for first-footers.

4 pints mild ale
1 tsp grated nutmeg
half-cup sugar
3 eggs
1 glass whisky

Gently heat the ale and nutmeg, and stir in the sugar. Beat the eggs; add gradually to the beer, stirring to avoid curdling. Add whisky to the mixture and heat gently, without boiling. Serve it in heated tankards.

"I like my whisky old and my women young."
Errol Flynn

Auld Lang Syne

ROBERT BURNS 1759–96

Should auld acquaintance be forgot,
and never brought to mind?
Should auld acquaintance be forgot,
and auld lang syne?

Chorus:
For auld lang syne, my jo,
for auld lang syne,
we'll tak a cup o' kindness yet,
for auld lang syne.

And surely ye'll be your pint-stowp!
and surely I'll be mine!
and we'll tak a cup o kindness yet,
for auld lang syne.

REPEAT CHORUS

We twa hae run about the braes,
and pu'd the gowans fine;
but we've wander'd mony a weary fit,
sin auld lang syne.

REPEAT CHORUS

We twa hae paidl'd i'the burn
frae morning sun till dine;
but seas between us braid hae roar'd
sin auld lang syne.

REPEAT CHORUS

And there's a hand, my trusty fiere!
and gie's a hand o'thine!
and we'll tak a right gude-willy waught,
for auld lang syne.

REPEAT CHORUS

Burns Night

Celebrated on 25th January, Burns Night is a tribute to Scotland's national poet, Robbie Burns. This practice emanates from north of the border but Burns Night is celebrated all over the United Kingdom – it's an ideal opportunity to dispel the gloom of January with some eccentric traditions, hearty food and plentiful whisky.

*Cock-a-leekie Soup
(Serves 8-10)*

*4 chicken leg portions
2½lb/1kg leeks, sliced and washed (including the green bit)
12 prunes*

Put the chicken in a pan with 5pts/3l of water and bring to the boil. Skim off any scum and cook for half an hour at a gentle simmer.

THE PIPER
At large-scale Burns suppers the guests are piped in to the accompaniment of bagpipes. This will be a touch ambitious for most home entertainers, but some traditional Scottish music on the CD player will create the mood.

THE CHAIRMAN
This is the name given to the host/organiser. Once the guests are seated the chairman should formally welcome them and announce the upcoming entertainment.

THE SELKIRK GRACE
Also known as Burns's 'Grace at Kircudbright', this Scottish prayer is recited before the meal begins:

*Some hae meat and canna eat,
And some wad eat that want it;
But we hae meat, and we can eat,
And sae the Lord be thankit.*

THE GASTRONOMIC STAR
At a formal Burns Supper the haggis is piped in on a silver platter, accompanied by the chef, a whisky-person, and the person who will address the haggis. At a more modest entertainment, carrying the haggis aloft to the accompaniment of claps and cheers will be sufficient.

HAGGIS

The dish consists of cooked, minced sheep's offal mixed with suet, oatmeal, seasoning and encased in the sheep's stomach. Once stitched up, the stuffed stomach is boiled for up to three hours.

Make a cut in the haggis skin before it reaches the table to avoid an explosion!

Add half the leeks, prunes and seasoning and simmer for 90 minutes, then add the remaining leeks and cook for a further 30 minutes. Remove the chicken legs, discard the skin, then pull the flesh from the bones, shred it slightly and return to the pan. Heat through gently and serve.

The Bill o' Fare
A typical Burns supper would consist of the following

Starter
Cock-a-leekie soup

Main course
Haggis, neeps & tatties (swedes & potatoes)

Pudding
Clootie Dumpling or Tipsy Laird (a Scottish sherry trifle)

Cheeseboard with bannocks (oatcakes)
Accompanied by wine, ale and lashings of whisky

THE ADDRESS

The haggis-addresser should now embark on a spirited rendition of Burns's (long) poem 'Address to a Haggis': *Fair fa' your honest, sonsie face, Great chieftain o' the pudding-race!* ….

He/she then cuts along the length of the haggis releasing the filling.

THE TOAST

With the simple toast 'The Haggis', and raised glasses, the meal is ready to begin. (The haggis is taken back to the kitchen to be served on individual plates). It will re-emerge, served with traditional neeps and tatties.

THE ENTERTAINMENT

Readings of Burns's poems and performances of his songs are interspersed with an amusing speech outlining his life story and the toast 'To the Immortal Memory of Robert Burns!'

TOAST TO THE LASSIES!

Drawing on Burns's writing, the toast is a witty tribute to the women present.

THE FINALE

The 'Chairman' rises to his or her feet and then thanks all the guests before a boisterous rendition of 'Auld Lang Syne'.

Valentine's Day

Valentine's Traditions

Hand in Glove By the late 16th century, gloves became a traditional Valentine's Day gift for women. In fact, it became custom for a young woman to approach her man of choice and utter the verse: "Good-morrow Valentine, I go today; To wear for you, what you must pay; A pair of gloves next Easter Day." If a man sent a woman an unsolicited gift of gloves and she wore them on Easter Day, she was advertising a positive response to his romantic overtures. In your dreams... In the 18th century Englishwomen would pin five bay leaves to their pillows — four on the corners, one in the middle — on the evening before Valentine's Day. This was said to help them see their future husbands in their dreams. Sweet songs In the 18th and 19th centuries, children celebrated Valentine's Day by going door to door, singing songs and sometimes begging for treats, such as fruit, pennies and cakes:

"Morrow, morrow, Valentine, I'll
be yours if you'll be mine,
Please to us a Valentine."

The 14th of February is a day for love and romance. Gifts and cards are exchanged, long-concealed feelings are brought to light, and all over the country couples enjoy intimate dinners for two.

There are many legends surrounding St Valentine, who was certainly a Roman martyr, who helped Christian prisoners, and became known as a heroic and romantic figure. The origins of St Valentine's day may lay in attempts by the early Church to 'christianise' the pagan fertility festival of Lupercalia, which fell in the middle of February.

The oldest known valentine still in existence today was a poem written in 1415 by Charles, Duke of Orleans, to his wife while he was imprisoned in the Tower of London following his capture at the Battle of Agincourt. It was not until the 17th century, however, that Valentine's Day was popularly celebrated.

By the middle of the 18th century, it was common for friends and lovers of all social classes to exchange small tokens of affection or handwritten notes, and by 1900 printed cards began to replace written letters due to improvements in printing technology. Ready-made cards were a convenient way for people to express their emotions in a time when direct expression of one's feelings was actively discouraged. The advent of cheaper postage rates also contributed to an increase in the popularity of sending Valentine's Day greetings.

> "My bounty is as boundless as the sea, My love as deep; the more I give to thee, The more I have, for both are infinite."
>
> *Romeo and Juliet*, William Shakespeare

SAY IT WITH FLOWERS

During the early 1700s, Charles II of Sweden brought the Persian poetical art known as the 'language of flowers' to Europe. Floral dictionaries were published, enabling lovers to use gifts of flowers to exchange romantic secrets, while entire conversations could take place within a bouquet of flowers. The red rose, for instance, was believed to be the favoured flower of Venus, Roman Goddess of Love, and became universally accepted to represent passion, while tulips are understood to denote a declaration of love.

✳ Never buy bunches of flowers from the supermarket or garage.

✳ Mixed bouquets can look cheap if they aren't substantial and well-styled; buy a bunch of all one type of bloom or go for just a single colour.

✳ Don't overlook the importance of the card that accompanies a delivered bouquet – it is an important part of the present.

A Romantic Dinner for Two

You can avoid the manufactured romance of restaurants, with their Valentine's Day 'specials', by organising a cosy dinner for two. But choose your food carefully, or romance will soon be dissipated.

You may be anxious to impress a new partner, or inject a familiar relationship with new spice, but don't make the mistake of thinking that this inevitably involves laying on an elaborate, complex meal. Unless you're a very confident cook, you may find yourself feeling harassed and overwrought, and this will kill romance stone-dead.

Don't spend more time in the kitchen than at the table.

Make your table look inviting, with shiny cutlery, glittering glasses, and a vase of flowers. Think carefully about the lighting, and create a seductive mood with candles, tea lights, or strategically placed, and well-dimmed, lamps. Choose any background music carefully, and keep the volume low.

Romance will soon dissipate under a harsh, unforgiving light.

Think about your menu. You will want it to be easy to cook and serve, but it should feel like a special treat. Beware foods that are difficult to eat – most people don't look very seductive when they're trying to manage a plate of slippery spaghetti or dissecting a bony fish.

Choose foods that won't distract your love interest's attention.

Lay on plenty of treats – bowls of nuts and figs, delicious sensuous chocolate, and fine wine. This will encourage your partner to linger over the dining table, the conversation and your company.

> "Ah me! Love can not be cured by herbs."
> Ovid

Aphrodisiacs

ASPARAGUS
Nineteenth-century French bridegrooms were required to eat several helpings at their pre-nuptial meal. Seventeenth-century English herbalist Nicholas Culpepper wrote that asparagus 'stirs up the lust in man and woman'.

TRUFFLES
Highly-prized, highly-priced, highly-scented.

BASIL
It's said to produce a general sense of well being – some also say that it boosts a person's sex drive.

FIGS
The Ancient Greeks are said to have celebrated the seasonal crop of figs with ritual copulation.

CHOCOLATE
The chemicals phenylethylamine and serotonin in chocolate stimulate the pleasure points in the brain. Chocolate is banned in some monasteries.

COFFEE
Perhaps it's the energy boosting caffeine...

OYSTERS
Apparently Casanova ate 50 for breakfast. Their high zinc content is said to fuel desire, but beware – you either love or hate them. Serve with a glass of chilled champagne.

Oysters are best in months which contain the letter 'R', when the sea is coldest, so they're the perfect treat for February.

Romantic Manners

Dates are the currency of romantic life, the oil that keeps the wheels in motion. No matter how much you procrastinate – flirting in cyberspace, seductive phone chats, emailed exchanges – you will have to face the horrible truth at some point; without a face-to-face meeting your relationship is going precisely nowhere.

Old-fashioned chivalry will always show men up in a good light.

{ "I do like a little romance… just a sniff, as I call it, of the rocks and valleys… Of course, bread-and-cheese is the real thing. The rocks and valleys are no good at all, if you haven't got that." }

Anthony Trollope

THE REQUEST When asking someone out on a date, you can do it face-to-face, by phone, text or email. Choose a venue and take care of the booking and instructions (time, back-up plans). If you are doing the inviting it is up to you to make the arrangements.

THE TIMING Punctuality is important; being up to 15 minutes late is not a problem, but more than half an hour late may look rude unless you have a genuine excuse.

Use your mobile phone to communicate any changes in arrival time.

THE CONVERSATION The conversation should centre on safe topics such as work, hobbies and family. Listen carefully and make sure you each have equal opportunity to speak. Only offer heartfelt compliments.

THE PRIORITIES A date involves interacting with another person, not with a mobile phone. So switch your phone off at the outset; don't leave it on the table, don't fiddle with it, or accept calls.

Your date should never feel second-best to your technology.

THE BILL Paying the bill is the responsibility of the inviter, at least on the first occasion. As things progress it is fine to take turns settling the bill.

THE CHIVALROUS GESTURE It is polite for a man to ensure that his companion gets home safely. Either share a taxi, dropping the woman off first, or accompany the woman to her bus stop/front door/tube station.

Don't over-compliment — it will make the other person feel uncomfortable.

THE HIDDEN AGENDA Intense eye contact, lingering touches, physical proximity — these are your passports to a second date. Read the signs and react accordingly.

THE FOLLOW-UP If you think you like what you see, follow up swiftly with a text, email or phone call. Don't leave your date hanging around for days on end because you think it looks cool.

Follow up with a text or email that evening or the next day.

THE BRUSH-OFF Resort to the universal language of failed dates, "Thanks for a lovely evening — let's do it again some time", which is a sop to bruised egos, but promises absolutely nothing. If that elusive connection just hasn't clicked into place, stay polite.

Shrove Tuesday

Shrove Tuesday is the last day before Lent. Western Christian churches view it as a day to cleanse the soul, as well as to celebrate and indulge before the fasting of Lent. It is also colloquially known as Pancake Day, Mardi Gras and Fat Tuesday.

The term Shrove Tuesday came about as Christians would confess their sins and receive absolution in a ritual called 'shriving'. In turn, pancakes became associated with Shrove Tuesday because households would feast on foods that they would not eat during Lent, including fats, eggs and milk. So, with the addition of flour, celebrations came to include a dish that could use up all of these ingredients – pancakes.

Shrove Tuesday is always 47 days before Easter Sunday (Sundays are seen as a day of celebration so they do not count as part of the 40 days of Lent), so falls any time between early February and early March. Shrove Tuesday marks different celebrations around the world, including the final days of both the Rio Carnival in Brazil and the Carnival of Venice in Italy, which are always held on this day.

Perfect Pancake Batter
Ingredients
140g/5oz plain flour
200ml/7 fl oz milk
100 ml/3.5 fl oz water
2 eggs
Unsalted butter
Pinch of salt

Classic Pancake Toppings

Butter
Sugar and lemon
Maple syrup
Chocolate spread
Banana and ice cream

Method
Sift the flour and salt into a
large mixing bowl. Make a
well in the centre of the flour,
and break the eggs into it. Mix
together the milk and water
and start mixing the eggs and
flour together, steadily adding
the milk and water mixture.
Keep whisking till all the
liquid is added and you are left
with a smooth batter. Leave to
rest, in the fridge, for about
30 minutes.

FRYING SUCCESS

Melt a small knob of butter in the frying pan, making sure the whole surface is greased. Once the pan is hot, use a ladle to add two tablespoons of batter into the pan, tipping it to get a thin even covering. Cook the pancake for about 45 seconds before flipping and cooking for a further 30 seconds, until lightly golden.

FLIPPING SUCCESS

If you're feeling brave, try flipping your pancake halfway through cooking. Wait until the pancake will slide freely in the pan, and then give it a go. Only flip once or else you risk making your pancake go rubbery.

AMERICAN STYLE ANY TIME

American pancakes are a fluffier and smaller version of the traditional British variety, mainly through the inclusion of baking powder and sugar to the batter recipe. Some claim that they are easier to make and tastier too. Traditionally served with maple syrup and crispy bacon (try streaky or pancetta), they are likely to be a popular addition to the weekend family breakfast table.

RETRO CLASSIC: CRÊPE SUZETTE

This classic French dessert never fails to please or impress. Caster sugar, orange juice, orange zest and butter are combined over a high heat to form a syrupy, caramelized sauce. Freshly-made crêpes are folded into quarters, and the sauce poured over them. A generous splash of orange liqueur (usually Grand Marnier) is then added to a pan and ignited by tipping the pan into the flame of the gas. This flaming liqueur is then poured over the pancakes. *Voilà.*

{ "The laziest man I ever met put popcorn in his pancakes so they would turn over by themselves." }

W.C. Fields

"When hospitality becomes an art it loses its very soul."
Max Beerbohm

"A guest never forgets the host who had treated him kindly."
Orson Welles

The Perfect Host

Your home is the theatre in which you entertain your guests and if you're going to be a successful host you must spend some time on both presentation and stage management. Even the simplest supper party will be greatly enhanced by a well-laid and decorated table, and guests will be gratified to see that your tableware and glassware is fit for purpose. You don't have to be a wine snob to find red wine served in a champagne flute deeply discouraging. Backstage your kitchen is the centre of operations: if it is well-equipped with indispensable gadgets and utensils, well-organised and generously stocked with store-cupboard basics, cooking for guests will be a civilised pleasure, not a kitchen farce.

Place Settings

When it comes to laying the table, we all know the basics. However, attention to detail and a general knowledge of correct form and traditions will mean that you are well-prepared for that rare yet very special occasion when it really matters.

Cutlery should look classic – avoid anything too embellished or modern.

Most of us, over time, will end up owning two canteens of cutlery: one for everyday use (often stainless steel) and another for special occasions (often silver). The cutlery you need generally comprises large knives and forks, small knives and forks, and soup and pudding spoons. Cutlery must always be immaculately clean and spotlessly shiny; be careful of fingerprints when you are laying the table.

The diner works from the outside towards the middle as the courses are served.

Forks go to the left, and knives and soup spoons to the right. Pudding spoons and forks go above (with the fork underneath the spoon; the bowl of the spoon points to the left, the tines of the fork to the right). Everything should be evenly spaced, with the bottom of the handles forming straight line. It is customary to place a butter knife on a side plate to the left of the place setting. Wine glasses go at the top right-hand corner, accompanied by a water glass. Make sure there is enough space to comfortably fit the largest plate that will be used – retrieving your cutlery from under a hot plate can be awkward.

Traditionally, a place setting is approximately 50cm (20 inches) wide.

Name cards and seating plans can be over-elaborate and, nowadays, formal seating arrangements are rarely necessary. There are, however, a few practicalities that work well: the hostess (or host if he's on kitchen duty) sits at the end of the table nearest the kitchen and the host (or hostess) sits at the opposite end. Men and women are alternated and couples are always separated. It is considered bad luck to have thirteen diners around the table – a superstition dating back to the Last Supper when Judas Iscariot was said to be the thirteenth diner to take his place – so often an extra place is set to make fourteen settings around the table.

Wherever possible, alternate genders, and break up couples to ensure talk flows.

TABLE MATS

If you have a beautiful wooden table, you can show it off to its best advantage by using table mats – these will protect the wood from hot plates and can also be used to create a distinctive look. A cork-backed mat with a classic design looks traditional; woven fabrics can be chosen to complement the colour scheme of your décor and look much more informal.

A tablecloth will conceal a multitude of imperfections. If you're going for a formal look choose traditional white damask. For more informal occasions you can let your imagination run riot.

NAPKINS

Napkins can be laid either in the space where the dinner plate will go, or on the side plate. Linen or damask is the traditional choice for a formal dinner party – they should be folded into very simple shapes (squares or trinagles) – elaborate origami looks over-laboured.

For less formal occasions, you can opt for paper napkins and enjoy choosing from the wealth of options available.

FORMAL VS INFORMAL

The style of the table should reflect the formality of the occasion. For a casual Friday-night supper with friends, you may only be serving one course and cheese, so kitchen cutlery is suitable. Make sure you have a selection of china that can be used everyday, as well as being mixed and matched for social gatherings. On the other hand, for more formal dinner parties that demand a sense of occasion, only the finest silver and tableware will do. Choose a plain design to avoid it looking dated – good quality china will last a lifetime.

Drinkware

If you plan on enjoying your drinks, then make sure you choose the right glass. The design, shape and capacity all combine to enhance the experience for the drinker.

The choice is endless, but there are a few essential styles which will make for a well-stocked drinkware cabinet. Be prepared for every occasion, from cocktail hour and evening aperitifs to fine wines and post-dinner digestifs.

Most glasses can withstand a cycle in the dishwasher but, for the best finish and to maximise your glass's lifespan, wash by hand in warm water. Dry gently with a soft, clean glass cloth, and avoid twisting the stems.

If your glasses turn cloudy soak them in vinegar for an hour, then rinse.

Store glass carefully and never stack them inside each other. If the glass hasn't been used for a while, wash before use. Alternatively, if you just want to revive the sparkle, briefly hold the glass over bowl of very hot water and allow the steam to cover the glass – polish with a glass cloth until it is gleaming again.

A Glass for Every Occasion

HIGHBALL
A tall, tumbler-style glass used to serve drinks that are made up of a spirit and mixer; for example, gin and tonic or scotch and soda. The size of the glass allows for a generous serving of mixer, and plenty of ice.

TUMBLER
A short tumbler (also referred to as an Old Fashioned glass) that is typically used for whisky and drinks served 'on the rocks' (ice), as well as some cocktails. A good quality tumbler will be weighty with a heavy glass base.

COCKTAIL
Sometimes called a martini glass, the iconic stemmed v-shape of the glass allows it to be held by the stem and therefore keep the drink cool, but also enhances the aromas of the cocktail.

SOUR
A small goblet-shaped glass with a short stem used for the sour family of cocktails – a term used to describe drinks that are mixed using spirit, citrus and sugar.

SHOT
A glass designed to hold a single or double measure of spirit, depending on its size. Quantities vary from country to country but, in the UK, a single measure is 25ml, and a double 50ml.

BEER
A strong and durable jug glass, with handy anti-slip dimples on the outside. This old-fashioned style of pint glass is perfect for an ale.

LAGER
A stylish alternative to the smooth-sided pint glasses found in pubs, tulip-shaped lager glasses are small and elegant, perfect for women who enjoy a beer.

PORT/SHERRY
A tapered, stemmed glass that allows the nose on port to be properly appreciated, and is also the perfect shape and size for the unique flavour and aroma of sherry.

COGNAC
Also known as a brandy balloon or brandy snifter, brandy is served in a bulbous glass which, when cradled in the palm, warms the spirit, intensifying the bouquet and enhancing the flavour.

LIQUEUR
A small-bowled glass designed for delicate, elegant sipping. The size and shape of the glass allows for the enjoyment of a liqueur's distinctive aroma.

CHAMPAGNE
A narrow, long-stemmed glass (or 'flute') that can be held without warming the champagne; the shape of the glass is designed to reduce the surface area and, therefore, retain as much fizz as possible.

RED WINE
A big, round-bowled glass that allows for plenty of aeration to enhance the flavour and bouquet; there are different styles available to suit both Burgundy and Bordeaux wines.

WHITE WINE
A narrower, less bulbous glass that preserves the delicate aromas of white wine by allowing some, but not too much, aeration.

On the Table

The menu is planned, the fine china dusted off and the cutlery counted… now is the time to think about the rest of the table. From glassware and serving dishes to fingerbowls and napkins, every detail counts.

The table should have some decoration, even if it is very simple.

A circular table suits a single centrepiece, whereas a rectangular or oblong one can take a couple of features. Avoid anything too big or tall – guests don't want to have their view across the table obstructed. Flowers are always elegant, but keep it seasonal and, for a modern look, stick to a single variety of blooms. Candles and tealights create a cosy, flattering light.

Don't let flamboyant decorations or candles block your guests' view.

If you have eschewed a traditional white tablecloth make sure there are plenty of mats available for serving dishes, wine, glasses etc., especially if you are precious about preserving your tabletop. Napkins should always be provided and always be linen, except for impromptu or informal gatherings or dining al fresco when pretty paper ones will do.

Make sure your guests will have everything they need; think everything through.

If you decide to include some messy foods in the meal plan, then think about what your guests will need. Shell-on prawns, for example, require a fingerbowl per person. Water should be lukewarm, with a slice of lemon for freshness. They are placed to the front-left of the place setting to avoid the wine glasses. Equally, a bowl of mussels requires a bowl in which to deposit the shells – make sure your table is big enough to comfortably accommodate the extra crockery.

Even the finest home-chef should provide cruet and condiments.

Cater for all tastes and make sure there are plenty of suitable accompaniments on the table. Provide salt (always sea salt) and pepper (always freshly ground) and, if it is a sizable table, a couple of sets of cruet will ensure nobody's left waiting or without. Place serving dishes strategically so that they are within easy reach for everyone; don't forget to provide serving spoons. If bread is on the table, always provide butter (and a butter knife).

Cocktails

When it comes to cocktail-making, stick
to the classics for the cleanest and classiest
results. The quality of your ingredients and
equipment – spirits, mixers, fruit, ice, glasses
– are an essential factor if you're concocting
the finest cocktails.

Choose simple, elegant glassware, and make sure that the
glass isn't too thick. Always choose the right glass for the
cocktail (the recipe usually specifies) as it will enhance
both the flavour and drinking experience. Glasses should
be clean, dry and chilled. Ensure you have a plentiful
supply of ice; glasses should be packed full to ensure it
doesn't start to melt and dilute the drink.

If you're serving cocktails avoid an ice-crisis by buying bags of ice cubes.

Choose trusted and iconic brands of spirit; avoid anything
premixed or ready-flavoured. Sugar syrup is called for in
many recipes and is, therefore, an essential ingredient. Try
to source one that is made from cane sugar. Fruit should
be seasonal where possible, garnishes should be made up
fresh for each glass and citrus must be freshly squeezed.
Don't be afraid of using egg white too – it binds and
emulsifies the citrus and alcohol in citrus drinks.

THE DRINKS CABINET

ESSENTIAL EQUIPMENT
Traditional Manhattan
  three-piece shaker
Boston shaker
Hawthorne strainer
Fine strainer
Zester
Muddler
Long spoon
Hand squeezer
Sharp knife

ESSENTIAL GLASSWARE
Collins/highball
Rocks/tumbler
V-shaped cocktail
Tall-stemmed liqueur
Small cocktail/sour
Coupette/Margarita
Cognac balloon
Champagne flute

ESSENTIAL MIXERS
Tonic water
Soda water
Ginger ale
Bitter lemon
Lemonade
Orange juice

ESSENTIAL INGREDIENTS
Absinthe (distilled)
Apricot brandy (Eau de Vie)
Bitters (Angostura and
  orange)
Brandy (Cognac and
  Spanish)
Campari (bitters)
Crème de cassis
  (blackcurrant)
Crème de fraise
  (strawberry)
Crème de framboise
  (raspberry)
Crème de pêche (peach)
Gin (London and others)
Maraschino syrup (cherry)
Pastis (anise)
Rum (white and dark)
Tequila (agave)
Triple Sec (orange)
Vermouth (dry and sweet)
Vodka (authentic)
Whiskey (American/
  bourbon)
Whisky (Scotch and malt)

FIVE FAMOUS COCKTAILS

OLD FASHIONED
2 parts bourbon
2 dashes Angostura bitters
1 white sugar cube
In an Old Fashioned glass, stir the sugar cube and bitters together. Pack the glass with crushed ice and pour over the bourbon. Garnish with a twist of orange.

DAIQUIRI
1 part sugar syrup
2 parts lime juice
8 parts white rum
Shake all of the above vigorously and strain into chilled Old Fashioned or cocktail glasses.

MARGARITA
1 part tequila
1 part Cointreau (or any orange liqueur)
1 part lime juice
Place the above ingredients in a cocktail glass with crushed ice and stir to combine. The rim of the glass should also be rubbed with a mixture of lime and rock salt.

MARTINI
1 part Vermouth
2 parts best-quality gin
Stir ingredients in a glass with ice. Strain into a chilled cocktail glass and twist some lemon peel over the top (do not put the peel in the drink – just twist it to spray the top with the juices).
Serve with a stuffed olive on a cocktail stick.

TOM COLLINS
1 tablespoon sugar syrup
Juice of 1 lemon
80–120ml gin (2 double measures)
Stir all of the above together in a tall glass and add four ice-cubes. Fill with soda water, stir again, and serve immediately.

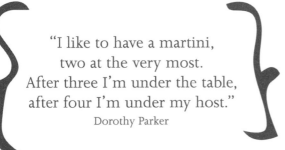

"I like to have a martini,
two at the very most.
After three I'm under the table,
after four I'm under my host."
Dorothy Parker

Aperitifs and Digestifs

A good host should be able to offer guests a selection of drinks before and after supper, and there are a few traditional choices that every household should stock. It goes without saying that when it comes to spirits it's best to stick to good-quality, well-known and classic brands.

APERITIF

This is a pre-meal drink that stimulates the appetite and palate. Traditional choices include chilled dry sherry, vermouth and Campari. Spirit-based drinks are also suitable; a cocktail, gin and tonic or vodka and a mixer. A simpler, and popular, option is a glass of chilled dry white wine or champagne.

DIGESTIF

This is a drink served after a meal; also known as a nightcap. Traditionally, digestifs are drunk to aid digestion after a large meal. They are usually strong and dark coloured spirits, such as brandy, Cognac and whisky. Fortified wines, such as port or Madeira, are also traditional options, as well as sweet liqueurs.

"There is no bad whiskey. There are only some whiskeys that aren't as good as others."
Raymond Chandler

WHISKY

SCOTCH SINGLE MALTS

The most prized bottles of Scotch whisky are single malts; these are produced from malted barley at a single distillery in Scotland. There are six recognised regions – Speyside, Lowlands, Highlands, Islay, Campbeltown and Islands – and each has its own distinctive style and character. Single malts are not to be confused with blended malt (previously referred to as 'vatted' or 'pure' malts).

RUM

A bit like Scotch single malts, the flavour and qualities of different rums depends on their origin. Most rums are made from molasses, but *rhum agricole* (from the French Caribbean) is made from fermenting sugar cane juice. White rum and light golden rums are best in cocktails; for a digestif choose a good-quality, aged, dark rum that deserves to be savoured and sipped.

COGNAC

Cognac (French grape brandy) has different grades depending on its age. V.S. (Very Special) is the youngest, having been stored for a minimum of two years in cask; V.S.O.P. (Very Superior Old Pale) is stored for at least four years but is often much older; XO (Extra Old) is the oldest. It must be stored in cask for a minimum of six years but, on average, is at least 20 years old. Some of the best (and most expensive) Cognac is an XO from a single-estate.

PORT

Port is a sweet, fortified wine from the Douro region of Portugal; it is traditionally drunk with cheese or after a meal. Bottle-aged port spends little time in a cask, whereas cask-aged ports mature in wooden barrels until they are ready to drink. It is wine to be laid down, as a cask-aged port that spends two years in a barrel will last 20–40 years in a bottle. It is best to drink vintage port.

Whisky from Scotland is spelt without an 'e'; from elsewhere it's spelt whiskey.

HOW TO DRINK WHISKY

Whisky should be drunk however you like it best. Adding water to a single malt is no longer frowned upon by the cognoscenti, but adding ice is still thought by many to interfere with the aromas. Diluting blended whisky with soft drinks, such as lemonade or ginger ale, is acceptable. Bourbon is also often drunk with a dash of water.

PORT ETIQUETTE

If a port decanter is placed on the table, help yourself and then pass it on, always to the left. If the decanter passes you by without your glass being filled, never attempt to ask for the decanter, thereby making it change direction. The decanter must return to the host without being put down. The tradition of passing the port originates from naval dinners where the port was always passed 'port to port' around the table – i.e. to the left.

SCOTCH WHISKY

In order to be classified as a Scotch, the whisky must have been produced at a distillery in Scotland; made from a mash of cereals; matured in an oak cask (in Scotland) for at least three years; bottled at a minimum of 40% A.B.V.

Champagne

Symbolic of celebration and success, champagne never fails to get the party started. Whether it's a few romantic glasses à deux, or dozens of bottles for a party, there is a right and wrong way to open and enjoy a bottle of fizz.

It is estimated that there are around 45 million bubbles inside a bottle of champagne.

ORIGINS

The Champagne region of France is situated about 90 miles northeast of Paris; its northerly position means that it is the country's coolest wine region. Champagne is divided into regions, but the majority of vineyards are situated in La Valleé de la Marne, near Reims and Epernay. There is a select group of 24 of the best Champagne houses, known as *Grandes Marques*.

RULES

Champagne is governed by numerous exacting rules that aim to maintain the highest standards, including: the wine must only come from the Champagne region, the vines must be grown and pruned in a specific way and the grapes must be picked by hand.

HISTORY

Made from a combination of Chardonnay, Pinot Noir and Pinot Meunier grapes, it is rumoured that a monk, Dom Pérignon, in the village of Hautvillers, first invented champagne in 1668 by accidentally discovering how to create a fizz in wine. *Méthode Champenoise* is the the process that creates the bubbles; adding a solution of sugar and yeast to wine creates a second in-bottle fermentation.

HOW TO OPEN A BOTTLE OF FIZZ

Ensure that it hasn't been shaken.
Peel off the foil over the cork.
Point the bottle away from you.
Remove metal cage over the cork.
Hold the cork in one hand.
Hold the bottle in the other.
Gently twist the bottle (not the cork).
Aim for a sigh not a pop.

HOW TO STORE

Ideally, bottles of champagne should be stored horizontally, but it is more tolerant of vertical storage than wine. Find a dry, dark place with a consistent, cool temperature. Non-vintage champagne is generally released for immediate drinking rather than cellaring, so don't hesitate before popping the cork…

HOW TO SERVE

Champagne should be served chilled (optimum temperature is about 7°C), in tulip-shaped flutes that are held by the stem (to avoid the heat of one's hands warming the champagne through the glass). Glasses must be scrupulously clean – even the most minuscule remains of washing-up liquid can cause the champagne to lose its fizz. The sign of a good champagne is a consistent stream of small bubbles that create a light froth on top, which is called the 'mousse'.

VINTAGE OR NON-VINTAGE?

Vintage champagne comes from the crop of a single year. A vintage bottle, therefore, always has a date on its label. A champagne house will only produce vintage champagne from very good years, and will typically release it after about six years. Non-vintage (NV) champagne is blended from the crop of different years; therefore there will be no date on the label. To fulfil the necessary requirements, vintage champagne must be aged for 36 months, and non-vintage for 15 months.

Size Matters

Piccolo ¼ bottle
Demi ½ bottle
Standard 1 bottle
Magnum 2 bottles
Jeroboam 4 bottles
Rehoboam 6 bottles
Methuselah 8 bottles
Salmanazar 12 bottles
Balthazar 16 bottles
Nebuchadnezzar 20 bottles
Melchior 24 bottles
Solomon 28 bottles
Sovereign 33.3 bottles
Primat 36 bottles
Melchizedek 40 bottles

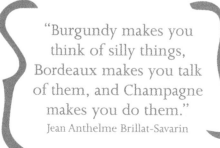

{ "Burgundy makes you think of silly things, Bordeaux makes you talk of them, and Champagne makes you do them."
Jean Anthelme Brillat-Savarin }

All About Wine

Most of the time, we know what wines we like to drink and, on a day-to-day basis, don't indulge in the finest bottles. However, it is easy to get stuck in a wine rut. Widen your horizons by trying wines from different regions and countries, as well as laying down some better bottles for a special occasion.

HOW TO STORE WINE

Wine that is to be kept for longer than a few months should ideally be stored in constant conditions, in the dark and away from vibrations at a temperature of 12–13°C (55°F). Sudden changes in temperature – such as rapid increases and decreases caused by central heating – can damage wine. Bottles should be laid on their side; this keeps the cork moist. Screw tops are becoming more common, especially for white wine, but it is generally accepted that very fine wines will always have corks.

BUYING EN PRIMEUR

When wine is bought en primeur (known as 'futures' in the USA), it is bought while it is still in the barrel, before it is released to the market. People buy wine like this to secure the best price; value can change considerably if a particular vintage gains status. Additionally, the exact size of bottle desired can be ordered, from half-bottles to magnums, jeroboams or larger. The bottled wine is then delivered to a bonded warehouse, where it is described as being 'in bond'; this really refers to a tax status as the wine is VAT and duty-free at that stage. Purchasers can keep their wines here until ready to drink (they often offer excellent storage conditions) or elect to take delivery sooner, at which point VAT and duty are paid.

KEEP IT SWEET

Sauternes in southern Bordeaux produces some of the best sweet wine in the world. The area's mists and sunshine encourage the growth of *botrytis cinerea*, a mould that dehydrates and, in the process, sweetens the grapes. Fans of dessert wine should also try Hungarian Tokaji and Italian Vin Santo.

TEN BORDEAUX CHÂTEAUX

Château Ausone
Château Cheval Blanc
Château Haut-Brion
Château Lafite Rothschild
Château Latour
Château Lynch Bages
Château Margaux
Château Mouton Rothschild
Le Pin
Pétrus

Principal Wine Countries

FRANCE is generally considered to be the most important wine-producing country in the world. The most famous regions are Bordeaux and Burgundy. The majority of wine from Bordeaux is red; in the UK, red Bordeaux is called 'Claret'. The region is divided by the confluence of the Dordogne and Garonne rivers with the Gironde Estuary; there are two main areas – the Left Bank and the Right Bank. The wines are generally blended from Cabernet Sauvignon and Merlot grapes. Burgundy is renowned for its sensual red and white wines, made respectively from the Pinot Noir and Chardonnay grape. The region's complex geography and geology, along with numerous producers and vineyards, mean that the wines vary widely in style.

ITALY produces excellent red wine, including the world-famous Barolo and nearby Barbaresco made from the Nebbiolo grape in Piedmont. Tuscany boasts an array of Sangiovese-based wines such as Brunello di Montalcino, Rosso di Montalcino and Vino Nobile de Montepulciano. Also try wine from the Chianti region (look out for bottles marked Classico or Riserva).

SPAIN is famous for its full-bodied, chunky red Rioja; also look out for elegant reds from Ribera del Duero (made from Tempranillo). For either, the grandest tend to be the Reservas or Gran Reservas. For white, opt for a crisp Verdejo from Rueda.

PORTUGAL produces the refreshing, spritzy white Vinho Verde, as well as some powerful, earthy and highly-flavoured reds.

GERMANY is most famous for Riesling; a perfumed and complex white offering degrees of sweetness and dryness.

SOUTH AFRICA boasts both excellent reds and whites; the most famous varieties are Chenin Blanc (a dry yet full-flavoured white), and their own speciality, Pinotage (an aromatic, spicy and full-bodied red).

CALIFORNIA is blessed with good geographical conditions and huge quantities of wine are produced there. Cabernet Sauvignon and Chardonnay are most famously associated with Californian wines, but look out for perfectly perfumed Pinot Noir, and elegant yet robust Zinfandel.

AUSTRALIA is the home of commercial 'New World' wines, and is well known for its Cabernet Sauvignon and Chardonnay. However, climate and geography allow Australian winemakers plenty of variety, so also try some excellent Shiraz (red) and Semillion (white).

NEW ZEALAND has a climate and geography that provides perfect growing conditions and the country produces some excellent wines. Its Sauvignon Blanc is considered to be amongst the finest white wines in the world; also look out for outstanding Pinot Noir.

CHILE is blessed with a viticulturally perfect climate, allowing a wide variety of grapes to thrive. Chilean wines are consistently good quality and well-priced – try excellent Cabarnet Sauvignon, Syrah and Pinot Noir, as well as outstanding Sauvignon Blanc and Chardonnay.

ARGENTINA is the home of excellent and well-priced reds; the main wine-producing region is Mendoza. Argentina is most famous for Malbec, a powerful and spicy red. Equally, the climate allows for some excellent Chardonnay.

Serving Wine with Food

When hosting a social occasion, as much time and thought should go into choosing the right wines as goes into planning the food. Bottles should be selected to complement the menu and, if you have a certified wine-buff coming over, then be prepared to open a decent bottle or two.

To be at its best, wine must be served at the right temperature.

Red wine should be served at 17–18°C (63°F), the temperature of a cool room. Fine white wine only needs 20 minutes in the fridge (including sauternes); too much chilling will hide the complexity of good wines. It's best, however, to chill cheaper bottles of white right down. On hot days keep bottles of white cool in an ice bucket – fill with a mix of ice and water, rather than just ice.

It is important to choose the right glasses for red and white wine.

A wine glass should be only one third full; it is better to underfill, rather than overfill, a glass. Reds should be served in a large glass with a bigger bowl to release the bouquet. Whites are served in a smaller, narrower glass that should always be held by the stem to avoid warming the wine (*see pp.152-3*).

Hosts should select the wines carefully and check them in advance.

A conscientious host will have selected wines in advance, so there is no need to open bottles you are given as a present if what you already have is more suited to the food. Hosts should check for any rogue corked bottles before pouring – if the wine is corked, it will smell musty, a bit like an old dishcloth. It goes without saying that you never smell the cork. Bits of cork (or sediment) in the wine do not indicate that the wine is corked.

Taste wine carefully; but there's is no need for dramatic gestures.

Simply swirl the wine in the glass, give it a sniff and take a small sip. Don't be intimidated by those self-proclaimed experts who demand to know which flavours you can detect. Smile, pronounce it delicious and avoid the question – at least you haven't fallen into the trap of making a boring exhibition of your ignorance.

DECANTING WINE

The process of decanting a red wine allows it to breathe. It separates mature wine from the sediment; it mellows and 'brings out' younger reds. Contact with the air livens it and, in a sense, 'accelerates' the ageing process. Decanting should take place a couple of hours before drinking but less, perhaps, for older wines that can fall away through the shock of air contact. Before decanting, ensure that the glass decanter is clean and soap-free. Pour the bottle at a reasonably rapid rate, being careful towards the end to ensure that any sediment remains in the bottle. Simply removing the cork from the bottle will not have the same (if any) effect; white wines are not usually decanted.

"Wine refreshes the stomach, sharpens the appetite, blunts care and sadness, and conduces to slumber."
Pliny the Elder

KNOW THE RULES
Drink white wine before red wine, and lighter wines before heavier ones. Complex food requires simple wine; simple food demands a more complex wine.

Coffee Break

From first thing in the morning until after dinner, coffee is the pick-me-up that punctuates most of our daily lives. Forget the quick fix of instant coffee – if you want to make the very best coffee, then you must invest in the right equipment and materials.

Take the time to make real coffee and savour a range of complex flavours.

Always brew your coffee on demand – never leave it sitting in a jug on a hot-plate as the flavour will disappear and it will taste stewed and bitter. Equally, never add boiling water to coffee; ensure that it is several degrees under boiling point or the intense sudden heat will damage the bean. Unlike tea, coffee should be served in warm cups, with warm milk and brown sugar. Cups and spoons should be small; an espresso cup should be the shape of half an egg and only filled up to two-thirds capacity.

Source your beans carefully and store them correctly.

Find a coffee bean supplier who can tell you where your beans are from, and how and when they were roasted. A grinder is a good investment as you can then grind your beans on demand, maximizing freshness. If you don't have one, ask your bean supplier to grind your beans for you. Many coffee suppliers add a helpful strength guide (1–5); 1 is very mild and 5 is dark-roast and strong.

Always have decaffeinated coffee to offer guests who fear being kept awake.

Store your coffee in a dark, air-tight container (oxygen and light ruins the flavour) – the fridge or freezer are the best places, and there is no need to defrost them before use.

The machinery you use should suit your preferred taste and style.

The ultimate coffee-making equipment is a home espresso machine. However, this may not suit everyone, and a cafetière provides not only a more practical option, but also some of the richest home-brewed coffee. Use dark roast beans – two scoops of coarse ground coffee per person is usually about right. Stovetop espresso makers are quick and easy (they require fine-ground beans), and will produce a thick, strong cup of coffee. Capsule or pod machines are clean, quick and convenient, but you are limited to the manufacturer's coffee, and they are therefore more expensive to run.

Coffee Know-How

BEANS AT A GLANCE

Caribbean: Jamaican beans are mild and sweet; Cuban and Puerto Rican are subtle, dark and intoxicating.

Central America: The coffees grown in Costa Rica and Guatemala are praised for their fine balance between acidity and sweetness.

Ethiopia: There are two main types: Harrar, generally considered to be finer of the two, and the gamey Djimmah. (Yemen offers excellent quality beans of a similar taste.)

Kenya: Kenyan beans are acidic with a full-bodied flavour and are of a consistently high standard.

Indonesia: These coffees are earthy, full-bodied and powerful. Arabica coffee from the island of Java is highly prized.

South America: Brazil and Colombia produce excellent rich and sweet beans; South American beans are usually a safe and reliable choice.

ALL IN A CUP

Americano: an espresso topped up with water.

Café crème: French coffee served with milk (similar to café au lait).

Café au lait: French coffee mixed with boiled (not steamed) milk, usually drunk at breakfast time.

Cappuccino: an espresso topped up with the same amount of steamed milk and then a similar amount of foamed milk. Sometimes, chocolate powder is shaken on top. A breakfast drink.

Espresso: hot water is forced, at high pressure, through ground beans, creating the purest coffee.

Flat white: less milk than a latte, folded into a double shot of espresso.

Latte: an espresso topped up with steamed or foamed milk. A breakfast time drink.

Macchiato: an espresso with a small amount of hot milk.

Mocha: a drink that includes both coffee and chocolate. (Mocha is also an extremely rare and fine bean from Yemen.)

PERFECT ESPRESSO

An espresso is not an espresso without an oily, golden crema – the layer of foam that floats on top of the coffee. Notoriously elusive to achieve at home, it should be able to support the weight of half a teaspoon of sugar for at least a few seconds.

Crema should not be yellow or creamy. An off-white and thin crema indicates that the beans need to be more coarsely ground and packed more tightly into the machine. A dark, burnt-looking crema means that the beans are too coarsely ground and tightly packed.

Essential Kitchen Equipment

There may be a gadget and a gizmo for
every ingredient and cooking technique,
but the accomplished home chef will not be
entirely dependent on a battery of high-tech
equipment and will be happy with a good
range of tried and tested everyday utensils.
Everyone, inevitably, has a favourite knife,
chopping board, pot or pan. Invest, wherever
possible, in better quality equipment – it will
have a longer lifespan and will withstand
daily wear and tear.

Knives are the most vital tool in the chef's arsenal; keep them well-sharpened.

COOKWARE

Cake tins (assorted)
Frying pans (big and small)
Griddle pan
Saucepans: large, medium,
   small, spare
Roasting tin for joints of
   meat
Low-sided roasting tray
   (large and small)
Sauté pan (high-sided
   frying pan)
Wok

ELECTRIC

Electric scales
Four-slice toaster
Kettle
Food processor
Meat thermometer

FABRIC

Apron
Cloths
Glass cloth
Oven gloves
Tea towels

DRINK

Cafetières (large and small)
Coffee bean grinder
Espresso machine
Ice bucket
Ice trays
Stove-top espresso maker
Teapot

ON A ROLL

Baking parchment
Cling film
Freezer bags
Kitchen roll
Tin foil

UTENSILS & EQUIPMENT

Can-opener
Cheese grater
Chinese bamboo steamer
Chopping boards
Colander
Knives
Measuring jug
Measuring spoons
Oil brush
Palette knife
Peeler
Pestle and mortar
Piping bag and nozzles
Potato masher
Potato ricer
Rolling pin
Rubber spatula
Salad spinner
Scissors
Sieve
Slice
Slotted spoon
Tongs
Whisk (flat and balloon)
Wooden spoons
Zester

KNIFE DRAWER

Serrated carving knife
Large chef's knife (approx
   20cm)
Meduim chef's knife
   (approx 15cm)
Vegetable paring knife
Flexible boning knife
Cleaver (approx 18cm)
Ceramic steel
Whetstone

SHARPENING KNIVES

For precise, easy cutting, you'll need sharp steel-bladed knives that are regularly maintained to keep a razor-like edge. The best results come from using a whetsone, available in different degrees of abrasion, generally divided between rough, medium and finishing. Good results can be achieved with just a medium stone, although a finishing stone will elevate the sharpness noticeably.

To sharpen your knife, put the whetsone on a flat surface and then place the heel (handle) end of the blade on the stone at an angle of 20 degrees, facing away from you. Push away in a long, sweeping arc across the stone and up to the tip of the blade, ensuring you keep a consistent angle. Repeat evenly and equally on both sides of the knife until the blade is really sharp.

Use a steel to maintain your knives. Hold the steel vertically with the tip placed on a surface. Place the heel of the blade at a 30-degree angle against the top of the steel and sweep the blade downwards. Maintain the same angle and apply light pressure in a smooth arc. Repeat several times on each side of the blade.

Essential Kitchen Cupboard

Every kitchen should have a well-stocked fridge and a wide-ranging ingredients cupboard. Whether it's for a quick weekday supper, an impromptu dinner with friends or a more formal occasion, a well-prepared home chef will be able to produce an impressive meal with ease and minimal fuss.

IN THE FRIDGE
Bacon, butter, cheese (including parmesan), crème fraîche, eggs (free-range), fresh herbs (including basil, thyme, flat-leaf parsley, mint and coriander), ginger (root), lemons, limes, milk, pancetta, potatoes, salad, vegetables.

IN THE FREEZER
Bread, broad beans, butter, chicken (thighs and fillets), milk, pastry, peas, prawns.

IN A JAR
Asafetida, bay leaves, bouquet garni, caraway seeds, cardamon pods, cayenne pepper, celery salt, chilli powder, chillies (dried), cinnamon sticks, cloves (whole), coriander (ground and seeds), cumin seeds, curry leaves, fenugreek seeds, fennel seeds, garam masala, juniper berries, lime leaves, mustard seeds, nutmeg, oregano, poppy seeds, saffron, sesame seeds, star anise, turmeric.

DRINK
Tea bags, loose-leaf tea (Earl Grey and English Breakfast), coffee beans (or freshly ground), herbal teas (a selection of flavours), fruit juice, squash and cordials, sparkling water, tonic water, soft drinks.

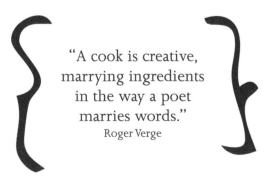

"A cook is creative, marrying ingredients in the way a poet marries words."
Roger Verge

IN THE CUPBOARD

Anchovies (in olive oil)

Baked beans

Baking powder

Bicarbonate of soda

Biscuits (sweet for tea, savoury for cheese)

Capers

Cashew nuts (unsalted for cooking)

Chocolate (70% cocoa solids)

Cocoa powder (70% chocolate)

Couscous (or quinoa)

Dried fruits (raisins, cranberries, apricots etc)

Fish sauce

Flour (plain, corn, self-raising)

Garlic

Gelatin

HP Sauce

Worcestershire Sauce

Marmite (unless you hate it)

Mustard (English, Dijon, wholegrain, powder)

Noodles (dried)

Oils (olive oil [extra virgin and standard], sunflower, sesame)

Olives (black)

Onion (white and red)

Oyster sauce

Pasta (penne, spaghetti, linguine, tagliatelle, orecchiette)

Peanuts (unsalted for cooking)

Peppercorns (whole black for grinding)

Pickle

Pine nuts

Plum tomatoes (tinned)

Porcini (dried mushrooms)

Rice (arborio, basmati, long grain)

Sardines

Sea salt (flaked and for grinding)

Soy sauce

Stock cubes (selection)

Sugar (brown, white, caster)

Tomato ketchup

Tuna (in olive oil)

Vegetable bouillon powder (stock)

Vermouth (dry)

Vinegar (balsamic, malt, red and white wine)

Yeast (sachets)

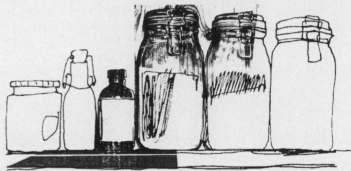

Index

Weights and Measures

WEIGHTS			DIMENSIONS			VOLUME	
Imperial	**Metric**		**Imperial**	**Metric**		**Imperial**	**Metric**
½ oz	10g		⅛ inch	3 mm		½fl oz	15 ml
¾ oz	20g		¼ inch	5 mm		1fl oz	30 ml
1 oz	25g		½ inch	1 cm		2fl oz	55 ml
1½ oz	40g		¾ inch	2 cm		3fl oz	75 ml
2 oz	50g		1 inch	2.5 cm		4fl oz	120 ml
2½ oz	60g		1¼ inch	3 cm		5fl oz	150 ml
3 oz	75g		1½ inch	4 cm		(¼ pint)	
4 oz	110g		1¾ inch	4.5 cm		8fl oz	240 ml
4½ oz	125g		2 inch	5 cm		10fl oz	275 ml
5 oz	150g		2½ inch	6 cm		(½ pint)	
6 oz	175g		3 inch	7.5 cm		16fl oz	480 ml
7 oz	200g		3½ inch	9 cm		1 pint	570 ml
8 oz	225g		4 inch	10 cm		1¼ pint	725 ml
9 oz	250g		5 inch	13 cm		1¾ pint	1 litre
10 oz	275g		5¼ inch	13.5 cm		2 pint	1.2 litre
12 oz	350g		6 inch	15 cm		2½ pint	1.5 litre
1 lb	450g		6½ inch	16 cm		4 pint	2.25 litres
1 lb 8 oz	700g		7 inch	18 cm			
2 lb	900g		7½ inch	19 cm			
3 lb	1.35kg		8 inch	20 cm			
			9 inch	23 cm			
			9½ inch	24 cm			
			10 inch	25.5 cm			
			11 inch	28 cm			
			12 inch	30 cm			

OVEN TEMPERATURES

Gas Mark	°F	°C
1	275°F	140°C
2	300°F	150°C
3	325°F	170°C
4	350°F	180°C
5	375°F	190°C
6	400°F	200°C
7	425°F	220°C
8	450°F	230°C
9	500°F	240°C